EMBRACING YOUR PERFECTIONIST SELF:

A Satirical A–Z Guide on Finding Comfort and Inspiration in Being Good Enough

EARLY PRAISE

"As an author and fellow perfectionist, this book speaks to me! By weaving together personal stories, interviews, and research in short manageable chapters, each with a different theme, Vanessa has shown us that perfectionism doesn't have to be eradicated completely. Instead of trying to exorcise it from our vocabularies, we can learn to harness our emotions, intelligence, and boundaries in constructive ways that actually serve us well. Vanessa brings a unique and refreshing perspective to something that afflicts so many, making us feel comfortable to be ourselves. A truly inspiring read!"

—LINDSEY POLLAK, *NEW YORK TIMES* BEST-SELLING AUTHOR AND CAREER AND WORKPLACE EXPERT

"I love the format because it's digestible, vulnerable, and playful. The A–Z chapters work very well through a combination of claims, data, and anecdotes. It is raw and powerful. Vanessa has created something that will impact generations to come. Get your copy now!"

—SUZAN BRINKER, CEO AND COFOUNDER OF VIV HIGHER EDUCATION

"I'm clearly a perfectionist, and I need to embrace that! I'm all for the satirical take as well. Can't wait to read it!"

—KAITLIN MATTES, HOME DESIGN DIY EXPERT AND HOST OF "HORRIBLY FLIPPED HOUSE"

Embracing Your Perfectionist Self:

A SATIRICAL A–Z GUIDE ON FINDING COMFORT AND INSPIRATION IN BEING GOOD ENOUGH

VANESSA BUSH M.ED.

MANUSCRIPTS PRESS

MANUSCRIPTS PRESS

EMBRACING YOUR PERFECTIONIST SELF:
*A Satirical A–Z Guide on Finding Comfort and
Inspiration in Being Good Enough*

ISBN   979-8-88926-770-6 *Paperback*
979-8-88926-771-3 *Ebook*

To my boys, Brayden and Benson—I hope you can see Mommy isn't trying to be mean or scary sometimes. She just wants the best for you. My hope is that you learn resiliency, that life doesn't have to be perfect, and that you can fall down and slip up and still turn out just fine. I want to encourage you to explore as much as you can. Never stop being curious. To me, you both are absolutely perfect, just the way you are.

To my husband, Kyle—thank you for never giving up on me, even when I gave you plenty of reasons to. You stayed, you forgave, you encouraged, and you continued to support and love me. I know it wasn't easy, so thank you from the bottom of my heart. I love you.

To Mom, Dad, and Bri—thank you for always believing I was a strong writer and that my stories were worth telling and sharing. You all stuck by me during those challenging and hard times, even when I drew back and pulled away. Thank you for your encouragement and forgiveness.

To Grandad—you'd be so proud I'm finally publishing something and putting it out in the world where it should be. You were so passionate about education and creating something meaningful, and I'm really glad you encouraged me to write and not worry about if it was perfect or not. I know you're having a beer in heaven and cheering me on.

Last but certainly not least—this book is dedicated to each and every one of you. Despite your challenges, struggles, shortcomings, or fears, believe you are wonderful and worthy. Humans are imperfect by nature, and you are, in fact, good enough.

Trigger warning:

*This book contains discussions of mental health issues that may
be distressing to some individuals. Topics include self-harm,
depression, anxiety, suicide, and eating disorders. I advise
reader discretion for individuals who may be sensitive to these
themes or have experienced trauma related to such incidents.
Please take care of your emotional well-being while reading.*

TABLE OF CONTENTS

INTRODUCTION

If it were a perfect world, pencils wouldn't need erasers because we wouldn't make mistakes.

—VANESSA, AGE EIGHTISH

I was late.

Somehow on the first day of third grade, the school bus missed my stop. Now I was already behind.

I was off to a good start.

Once I got to my classroom, I went into the closet to unpack my supplies for the day and hang up my backpack. So terrified of facing my peers and my teacher alone, I couldn't bear even to turn around. I kept loading and unloading my supplies. I became arrested in place, fear and anxiety running through my mind as sweat dripped down my face.

Eventually, my teacher realized I had been in there too long and called out my name in front of everyone—my worst fear.

"Vanessa, can you join us over here, please?"

Shaking and scared, I reluctantly walked out into the sea of desks, everyone's eyes on me, and finally settled into my chair.

I had never been so scared. Even today, that story still feels raw, real, and fresh.

What was I so scared of?

It turns out my perfectionism was to blame. I truly believed it was my own personal fault I was late to class, that I somehow could have prevented it. I became mad at myself, ashamed, and scared my classmates would make fun of me or judge me. Like so many others out there, my fear deeply rooted itself in my belief that I was an impostor, I was less than, I was imperfect.

I've felt this way all my life.

Growing up in an affluent suburb of Boston, Massachusetts, I've always been a Nervous Nellie. The community and culture I was born into encouraged me to believe that mistakes were bad, failure wasn't an option, and that I had to consistently strive for excellence. Enormous pressures, impossibly high standards, all within a hyperindividualistic environment. As a kid and now in my mid- to late thirties raising two young boys, I know perfectionism will always be a part of me.

The question now becomes—how can I use my perfectionist tendencies as strengths instead of weaknesses? What if I could learn to be more resilient and comfortable with change and the unknown?

How can I still be me, in a healthier form?

First, let's define perfectionism in the scope I'll be using throughout this book. The definition I found most helpful comes from UK psychologist Dr. Joachim Stoeber: "Perfectionism is a multidimensional personality disposition characterized by striving for flawlessness and setting exceedingly high standards of performance accompanied by overly critical evaluations of one's behavior" (Routledge 2017).

Okay, yikes.

As if that definition wasn't bad enough, it's on the rise, and things aren't looking good.

In 2017, Curran and Hill published a revolutionary study that measured the levels of perfectionism of over 40,000 college students from 1989 to 2016. They found the respondent rate almost doubled in size from 9 percent to 18 percent—telling us that something needs to shift fast.

When COVID-19 hit in early 2020, the world changed even further. We saw a lot of disease, destruction, devastation, and depression. In April 2022, Mental Health America found overall increases in moderate to severe mental health crises largely due to the pandemic. In particular, youth, Black, and LGBTQ+ individuals were more negatively affected—scoring higher on screens assessing psychosis, anxiety, stress, depression, eating disorders, and suicide (Mental Health America 2021).

So what does this all mean?

Well, let me take you back to the summer of 2022.

I was in San Francisco at a work conference, enjoying the company of higher ed thought leaders from around the country. The view over the Golden Gate Bridge at the Presidio Park was otherworldly and serene, the sun peeking through the quintessential San Fran fog and tall trees swaying in the cool breeze.

One of our keynote speakers was Eric Koester, Georgetown professor and founder of the Creator Institute. He conducted a workshop where we shared projects we were working on or trying to work on, so we could see how the power of community could help get them done.

An article series I had been working on for the better part of fifteen years came to mind. A Word document capturing all my satirical ideas and advice to myself if I could relearn behaviors to help me manage my perfectionism. All my fears, realizations, learnings, and hopes from trying to deal with this disposition, this disease—I had never really shared it with anyone up until this point.

What would everyone think?

As I started talking with others, I realized I wasn't afraid anymore.

I don't know why it took that moment at the conference, but suddenly I felt I could finally let go. I decided to take my own advice and embrace the unknown and the unfinished. Feeling like a bit of an impostor among these impressive people, I still felt inspired and motivated. Everyone was supportive, many even volunteering their stories or wanting to be involved.

I decided I wasn't going to write alone. I wanted to tap into others' stories about this ailment affecting so many, paralyzing our decisions, and whispering we need to do it all and be the best. If current trends continue, a vast majority of the population will be woefully underequipped to meet life head-on, and we need these anecdotes to help us realize we're in this together.

One particular story felt ripe for sharing, given this cultural shift—my experience with anorexia. Growing up in the 1990s and 2000s, I felt models were razor thin and people judged you based on your weight and commented on your body and eating habits. I was affected pretty badly. College was a hell of a ride. Everyone measured by numbers and prized skipping meals.

This went on for the better part of fourteen years.

Fourteen miserable years.

It strained relationships, caused rifts, increased mental and physical stress, caused missed opportunities, and resulted in a massive despair and sadness cloud for too long. At that time, I did not have the tools to affirm I was still a person worth loving and knowing.

Luckily, I recovered.

Not everyone does.

So many anorexics suffer from this incessant need to be flawless. And it's exhausting.

I realized I didn't want to feel that way anymore, and I didn't want others to suffer either.

Given both the positive increase in mental health conversations and the depressing research trends out there, it seems like the right moment to share information and inspire others—family, friends, colleagues, strangers, type A personalities, enneagram type ones, and really anyone feeling lost and struggling to keep up with it all.

The purpose of this book is not clinical in nature. My intention is quite the opposite. I've been through therapy, doctors' visits, and tough conversations. Those made me scared, unlikely to open up, and I felt judged. I'd rather share stories, advice, and inspiration from the people who have been on the front lines. Those who have experienced perfectionism are better suited to give tips the rest of us can use.

It's time to learn from our peers—to rethink and reshape what success is, to allow failure and mistakes to happen without judgment, all to live a better, healthier, more fulfilled life.

It's time to use research to inspire, not to get bogged down and caught up in the data, but to help inform our next steps and encourage us to keep on going.

The ultimate goal of this book is to find common ground and build each other up. We need to be vulnerable, gain some perspective, and think alternatively to embrace who we are at our core. Rather than simply recover or overcome, I'm here to offer a different approach. We need to put in the work, stop running away, and learn to manage our tendencies in more constructive ways.

COVID-19, as ugly as it was, taught us mental health is important. We need to slow down and appreciate the important things in life. The world inherently is and always will be imperfect, like the human experience.

So here I am—bearing it all openly and unapologetically, not embarrassed or ashamed, ready to embrace accountability and change, committed to learning and failing forward and viewing all that as good instead of bad.

I don't want to change who I am. I want to be a better version of myself. And I have a feeling you do too.

I have over thirty years of practice at this. And shocker, I'm still not perfect and never will be. But as I mentioned, now feels like the right time to share all this. Not just because mental health is more recognized or perfectionism is on the rise, but because of my two little boys.

When I became a mom, I realized I never wanted my kids to feel how I felt growing up—scared, afraid, nervous, anxious. Hesitant to just be myself. I want to show them mistakes make us human. We don't always have to know our next move or be the absolute best all day, every day. I don't want them not to love who they naturally are. Because to me, and to the world, they are perfect.

Humans are natural storytellers, and I'm here to tell mine. So feel free to jump around as you see fit or stay buckled in for the whole ride. I hope this book can serve as a useful guide for you and maybe someone you know.

Remember, good can be good enough!

A

A IS FOR AMBITION

When we are young, we are told to go for our dreams and reach for the stars. Believe it and you can achieve it! So, when we get older and have more wisdom (read: life experiences), why are those phrases seemingly bullshit?

Is too much ambition a bad thing?

One of the greatest novelists of our time but perhaps one of the most tormented individuals of the twenty-first century, David Foster Wallace, was interviewed about this intersection of ambition and perfectionism. He was, of course, a strong and talented writer but certainly suffered from his share of struggles and perceived shortcomings. He noted, "You know, the whole thing about perfectionism... is very dangerous, because of course if your fidelity... is too high, you never do anything... It's actually kind of tragic because it means you sacrifice how gorgeous and perfect it is in your head for what it really is" (Farnam Street 2017).

This directly speaks to ambition's dark side—achievement versus avoidance. We suddenly delay doing anything (i.e., procrastinating) because we are so ambitious and want everything to be perfect, but we realize it is overwhelming and don't even know where to start. In many ways, before we begin, we stop.

Why is that?

An article in the Harvard Business Review explores this further: "In excess, ambition damages reputations and relationships and can lead to catastrophic failure" (Carucci 2021). Quite literally, we can become our own undoing. Further, "Thomas Curran and Andrew Hill's meta-analysis of rates of perfectionism from 1989 to 2016, the first study to compare across generations, found significant increases among more recent undergraduates in the US, UK, and Canada. In other words, the average college student last year was much more likely to have these tendencies than a student in the 1990s or early 2000s... This rise doesn't mean each generation is becoming more accomplished. It means we're getting sicker, sadder, and even undermining our own potential" (Ruggieri 2022).

Unfortunately, I know this all too well.

I spent so many of my formative years being sad, feeling alone, and wondering where I was going in life. While I was smart and got straight A's, I struggled to find my place in the world and know what it was I wanted to do. I envied those who knew the career path they wanted to follow, or really just anyone who seemed outwardly confident, projecting assurance and power. It was as if they understood how life worked and excelled at it. Even though I didn't feel that way on the inside, I still wanted to experience some semblance of self-confidence.

So what did I do? I got ambitious.

I was a true competitor in every sense of the word. Even as a kid growing up, I remember always needing to beat anyone at anything, whether it was a game of hide and seek, checkers, or who could jump the highest or run the fastest. In grade school and later in college, I felt I had to earn a break, that if I wasn't challenged enough or felt exhausted, I wasn't doing it right. An A was fine, but an A+ was better. With my body, I had to be the thinnest person around. Otherwise, I deemed myself a failure. I wanted to achieve 100 percent in every aspect of my life. Nothing was exempt.

But here's the trouble with that school of thought—I wasn't happy. Earning A+s and being rail thin did not solve those deep feelings of longing—to belong, to be loved, to be appreciated, to be validated, to be worthy. If anything, it alienated me from my closest friends and family.

So if ambition can make us sad, sick, and a social outcast, is there a positive side to it?

In speaking to Roger Osorio, an author who writes about reinvention and teaches entrepreneurship, he believed so. I asked him what his thoughts were on ambition, how it drives us to work on projects, and if it can ever hinder us.

He told me, "Perfectionism, to me, is an obsession to do well on something I'm excited about."

In this sense, ambition is mostly a good thing. It can challenge us, motivate us, and push us. But even he thinks ambition has its limits.

"I wonder, though, when is ambition a bad thing? When does it distract from other projects or deadlines I'm supposed to be doing?"

It's a fair point. In some respects, the desire to be ambitious and focus so intently on one thing inherently means something else is left behind. It can be helpful as long as it doesn't compromise other important things, like family, mental sanity, or perhaps just another project.

We can't excel at everything. It's just not possible. And that's okay.

I would argue a healthy dose is what can make you truly successful and help you stay focused and motivated. Anything from daily chores to long-term goals needs a little dash of ambition to drive us forward. The ability to strive, reach, and be excited along the way is, for the most part, a good thing. It becomes troublesome and borderline unhealthy when we get too far in the clouds and end up sacrificing something (our health, a relationship, a job, etc.) for this lofty ideal.

And when you accelerate it at lightning speeds, the result is less than suboptimal. We become stagnated, frustrated, and paralyzed by our own inability to get what we want or get where we want to go fast. That's the key here—perfectionists are used to being ambitious, that goes without saying, but it's when we fail to see mountains move at breakneck speed that we get irritated and even deterred from our original tracks. We can fall off, become upset, and then lose focus altogether.

We tend to think in very black-and-white terms. It's either right or it's wrong—zero to sixty. Go big or go home.

How many great leaders figured things out on the first try? Didn't Edison reportedly test one hundred ways to make a lightbulb? Only one needed to work, and he never gave up, even with one failure after another.

I had one of these moments a few years back when trying to change positions in my career. I felt stuck where I was and craved something more. I was ambitious, nearly to a fault. I expected something to come my way very quickly and without a lot of hard work. After all, I was successful in my career, had the credentials and experience to prove it, and had solid recommendations. There was just one problem—the job application process. One could argue that talented individuals oversaturate the higher education market in the Boston area. It wasn't me that was the problem. It was the process itself. Ever heard the expression, "Hate the game, not the player"? It was one of those scenarios where the inability to get what I wanted resulted from the process, not my qualifications or skills. Of course, I took it personally and got very frustrated and depressed. I was sad, thought nothing would come my way, and wallowed in self-pity.

Does this story sound familiar? Is too much ambition crushing your momentum?

I'd suggest changing it up.

I attended a workshop where I met a higher education marketing leader who, I learned, needed someone on her team. Afterward, we chatted for a bit, and she informed me about the qualifications and details. The role sounded appealing and what I was looking to get more involved in. I was delicate in the conversation at first, not wanting to sound desperate or one-track minded, and slowly inched the discussion toward my job search and what I was seeking. She helped me connect with her team, and the rest is history!

I say that, but in all honestly, it was the result of an extraordinary amount of hard work networking and attending all opportunities that presented themselves to me. I realized I needed to do more things outside my comfort zone and take more risks. If what I was doing wasn't working, then I needed to try something different.

I can look back on this experience and sum it up like this: Ambition is helpful but can be detrimental if you can't adjust your expectations or switch tactics. Ambition is at its best when you share it with others. Let them know what you want, how they can help, and how passionate and excited you are. Hard work and drive are both important, but those alone may not be enough. When you are ambitious, allow yourself time, patience, and perhaps some alternatives to get where you want to be.

A true tête-à-tête of drive and patience. Never was a battle won without a little bit of both!

B
B IS FOR BEING THE BEST

Have you heard of the phrase, "No good deed goes unpunished"?

Turns out, that's what can happen if you're trying to be the best all the time.

Here's an example—your colleague is doing exceptionally well at hitting team goals, and you and the rest of the team are falling behind. Everyone except for this rockstar appears to be slacking, and soon the manager gets involved and says those higher metrics are now the new team goals.

After all, if this one person can do it, everyone should be able to, right?

According to *Scientific American*, "Decades of research on social comparisons show that when we size ourselves up relative to people who are better than we are (or as good as we are) on a particular dimension, we are likely to experience discomfort, envy, or fear" (Gino 2017). Especially in the workplace, resentment and annoyance set in, and by association, that star employee has now become the perfect target.

With regards to perfectionists, we can become too tunnel-visioned where it's our way or the highway. We may hyperfixate on unattainable goals and forget other priorities that need our attention. This desire and magnetic pull toward wanting to outperform and beat our competition may even go so far as to predispose us to eating disorders, phobias, and even suicide. In short, striving for that perfect score can sometimes leave us with a big fat zero.

So what do we do about it?

Believing that we have it all figured out, aligned just right, with no room for errors or flaws, we can't possibly let someone else *beat* us because then that means we're not perfect. And, of course, that would be tragic, right?

Wrong.

Seems like there is a power struggle to consider here, as well as questioning who is the one that's defining best and how.

For example—a *best in show* award, according to who? Why? What were the criteria? Was there an ulterior motive?

Being the best requires us to think about biases. We all have them. It's a matter of asking ourselves these questions:

Who's asking and why?

What is the reason behind it?

Where is the line drawn?

Why does it matter?

One afternoon when my husband and I were both working from home, he became frustrated and came to me seeking advice and help. He kept mentioning he felt the need to be his absolute best all the time. He could never slip up or show weakness. On this particular day, he found a piece of work challenging and struggled to get out of his emotional rut. He didn't feel as though he was *on top of his game*, and that bothered him.

I asked him, "But why do you think you have to be the best out of everyone? Does doing well but not being the best mean you failed somehow?"

When I put it that way, he looked at me and said, "Yeah, I think so."

He looked super serious when he responded, so I assume he thought that if he wasn't performing at top-notch levels, they would fire him or something. That seemed to be his worst fear.

I asked him to go down this rabbit hole with me.

"Okay, so if you get fired, will your world fall apart? Will the kids still be okay? Will our house still be standing? Will your career be completely over?"

No. Yes. Yes. No.

"Exactly," I said. "Even if those fears manifest, we're still gonna be okay."

He considered this for a moment, looked up from staring at the floor, and said, "You know what, you're right. I don't think it's as bad as I'm making it out to be. I'm definitely hardest on myself."

Bingo.

And same, by the way.

When I met my friend Monica Quimby in college in 2005, I could tell she was one of those girls who just flew by the seat of her pants, and she epitomized the phrase *work hard, play hard*. A bit outside my comfort zone at first, she and I hit it off and have never looked back. She became one of the first people I met at the University of New Hampshire where I felt comfortable being myself, not embarrassed, not hiding anything, someone I could be my true self with. She made it possible for me to see I didn't have to be only a book nerd or only a social butterfly. I could, in fact, be both.

That first year we met, we went to parties together, traveled during winter break, danced on bars, ate each other's french fries at late-night diners, encouraged one another's dreams and aspirations and nerd goals, swapped growing up in small town stories, traded jokes, and just had an absolute blast together. We were quickly becoming soul sisters.

In late January 2006, almost six months into our newly minted friendship, we made plans to hang out after she returned from a school-sponsored ski trip. The hour when we were supposed to meet up came and went. I tried calling her cell, all to no avail. Oddly, I never heard back from her that night.

Turns out it was for a good reason. She had been in a major ski accident on her last run down the mountain. She went off a jump, got spooked and cut off by a snowboarder, and landed awkwardly, flipping and turning at breakneck speed—literally. She ended up severing her spinal cord.

To say her life changed in an instant would be an understatement.

For someone whose life was defined not only by her academic accolades and her sunny personality but her love and involvement in sports and activities, this was a devastating blow.

I recall getting the news the next morning at the dining hall from another friend. I couldn't believe it. Monica was in a coma and, according to the doctors, also paralyzed.

When I first saw her in the hospital bed, hooked up to breathing machines and IVs and looking nothing like the Monica I had come to know and love, I was devastated, but of course nothing compared to what I know she must have been feeling and going through. For an able-bodied, extraordinarily talented, and involved athlete, she suddenly found herself paralyzed and unable to do many of the sports she once loved in the same way.

It would take years and years of physical and emotional therapy as well as countless hours of introspection and redefining what her life would now mean to get her where she is today.

But like the Monica I first met, that spiciness and fire was still in her. I think these qualities, above anything else, were what ultimately saved her from spiraling down into a depressive slump—she refused to quit. Instead of viewing her injury as a complete tragedy, she reinvented herself and found new ways to do what she loved.

That also meant she could no longer be the best in the same manner she was used to. She had to relearn and retrain her body, tapping into different muscle groups and other strengths to compensate for the parts she couldn't use fully. Rather than seeing that as a failure or tragic loss, she saw them as learning opportunities. Especially in her role as an elite adaptive athlete, she understood being the best is not about the individual. In a team sport like hockey, "You are not the win. You are part of the win."

When we suddenly shift from believing that everything will crumble and fall apart if we don't do our absolute best to realizing life will carry on just fine, we can make progress. According to Dr. Jacob Towery at Stanford University, "If you develop a growth mindset, setbacks can become learning opportunities, and there is always another chance to improve and feel better" (Stanford University 2021).

Now how about that? We are still worthy. We are still doing a good job. We are still going to be loved.

Being the best at something doesn't signify you are worth more than someone else.

Being the top student doesn't mean there aren't other smart individuals out there.

Being the best athlete doesn't mean you are perfect at every sport, every exercise, every time.

Being the best mom doesn't mean other moms are doing it wrong or worse.

A mental health counselor once told me this incredibly simple and impactful nugget when I explained to her my rationale (read: excuse) for unnecessary worry, a.k.a. anxiety:

"Worry is a waste of time. The amount of worry does not impact the outcome."

Whoa.

Say that again for the people in the back: "Worry does not impact outcomes."

Being the best is nice in theory but doesn't usually serve us perfectionists well. It's reasonable to have intentions of doing your best and trying hard because you care or want to be loved and supported, understood, and just human. Most of us feel like that. Where we tend to go wrong is when we let being the best limit us, hold us back, and make us scared to try something different or new or scary. Funny enough, I feel the best things in life come from taking risks: love, marriage, jobs, families, etc.

Without testing how far we can go, how will we know all we can accomplish and achieve? How will we truly know our best if we don't challenge ourselves and allow mistakes and failures to teach us and help us grow?

Best, in this new definition, means giving yourself permission to redefine what success, achievement, and happiness all look like. Instead of being the best, perhaps it's just that we need to be comfortable and content with being good enough.

C
C IS FOR CONTROL

Nerd moment: Do you happen to know the origin of the word control?

While there are a few different versions depending on the language origin, generally speaking, control comes from *contra*, or against, combined with *rota* or wheel/roll.

Almost word for word, it's going against the roll, trying to manipulate the natural flow of things, arresting progress, or keeping something from moving ahead.

Perfectionists believe we're perpetually in charge and have power over our environment, other people, our actions, or ourselves. We somehow manage to forget that life is a series of happenstance events, unable to be manipulated or negotiated at our whim. And, of course, we believe we have the power to set the course for everything in life.

According to Theravive, "Perfectionism is about an almost obsessive need to have control over every aspect of... life. This need for control comes from a deep-seated shame regarding failure. As this is an unrealistic goal, it can create great feelings of anxiety and depression... They view simple mistakes as failures as opposed to learning experiences" (Theravive 2023).

If we want control, but that means we are depressed, then what's the point? Do we really think we need a regimented structure over every aspect of our lives? And if so, does that equate to happiness?

News flash: Jokes on us because, as Benjamin Franklin so famously said, "In this world, nothing is certain except death and taxes."

So why, then, do we attempt to go against the roll in every situation and believe we have the power to effectively, strategically, and successfully manage it?

I have tried to control nearly every aspect of my life since before I can remember. Delicately navigating through this racetrack called life, I have tried to consider my choices and paths carefully and to try and negotiate through them in a predictable way.

Most recently, I have learned the hard way despite doing everything right, you can still be blindsided by something unexpected and have no choice but to pivot and chart a way forward.

In 2020, as the world went to hell in a handbasket and life as we knew it was changing rapidly before our eyes, my then nine-month-old was suddenly diagnosed with food allergies. We suspected he might have been allergic to peanuts, but then we got a call after his blood test results came back. I'll never forget how I felt that day when they read off even more things I had to try to avoid with him: peanut, egg, sesame, lentil, chickpea.

Each word felt like a bullet to my chest.

I went numb. I cried. I panicked. I spiraled. I couldn't get to sleep most nights. I envisioned the worst. I created these microcosm environments of despair I could not overcome.

My husband and I were shocked and scared and honestly didn't know where to turn or how to manage. Nobody in our direct families had food allergies, and we were quickly thrusted into an unknown world that we had to assimilate to—unwillingly, but necessarily.

That year was extremely tough—COVID-19, the stress of navigating through sudden change on a global scale, my firstborn unexpectedly having food allergies, etc.

And it turns out we weren't alone. Many parents, mothers in particular, were found to bear the "primary responsibility for managing a child's food allergy and felt inadequately supported for doing so... mothers of food-allergic children had a poorer quality of life as well as higher levels of anxiety and stress than fathers" (Hewett 2020). Moms struggle with so much guilt. This just adds to it. Lucky us.

And hey, this is not to say all fathers are not feeling this burden. I know my husband felt and still does feel extreme guilt, as if we should have known better somehow that there were things we could have done to actively prevent him from this diagnosis. He's an analyst by trade and by personality, so reading into the data and dissecting every little detail is part of his inherent nature. He blamed himself for his son's allergies. It still feels raw for him, even today.

As a perfectionist, this was one of the most difficult times in my life. Maybe single-handedly, the most difficult.

Suddenly, control went out the window, anxiety ran rampant, nothing made sense, and I didn't have the tools to deal with it all. I couldn't fathom what the future looked like anymore. What I had previously known, how I had related and responded to the world, didn't seem to work in this situation. I felt blind, like I didn't know what the next steps were or how to go about my days. Control didn't mean anything anymore because it was out of my hands. Nothing I did seemed to make a difference. And that was truly scary. If I couldn't control anything, then what did that mean for me? Who was I now?

After some time, therapy, and talking with others who've been in this position before, I can now say we are managing to live with it. We are the one in thirteen diagnosed with food allergies (Food Allergy Research & Education 2023). We've come from the days of panic and tragedy to days where we are still cautious but living and thriving. His IgE levels (what doctors use to determine an allergy) have since dropped. If they trend downward over time, that's a good sign.

We are hopeful he will have true food freedom one day, but we also know others are dealing with this too. We have learned coping techniques and best practices and have even become mentors and experts in some regard. The power of community and education have been godsends for us here.

The lesson in all this seems pretty clear to me. Despite our desperate intentions to hold on to a *perfect* world, we absolutely have no control over every aspect of life. Even when we do things according to plan, they can still take a turn and go wrong. What does that even really mean? Trying to control everything is a waste of time.

It's like I'm trying to justify the worry sometimes, as in, "I worried all day and stressed so much. The universe should reward me and lessen my anxiety load." Intently worrying will make a positive difference if I just freak out hard enough, right?

No clue why I think this way, but as I get older I'm realizing more and more it doesn't serve me.

I'm trying to get better at this, recognizing that my anxiety and need to control the situation won't impact what will actually happen. That worry can turn into a literal and metaphorical loss of energy. I could instead be focusing on the aspects of life I do have control of (or at least a semblance of it) and recognizing the areas where I just don't.

So go easy. Let go more. Get comfortable with being uncomfortable. Realize the world has managed just fine without us and will continue to do so. Control is for the birds.

D

D IS FOR DISCOVERY

When we peel back the layers of someone's personality, we may find something unexpected, something perhaps unbeknownst even to them. I can think of a few people who aren't very self-aware and can't budge or reason with anything other than their point of view.

They may be so entrenched and engrossed in their ways they cannot look past it and see any other potentially valid way.

Perfectionism can be a lot like that, masking what lies beneath.

For so many years growing up, I thought life operated in the black and white spaces, not the murky, muddy, messy gray waters in between. It wasn't until college I realized life didn't follow a playbook where you could look up the rules, follow them, and predict the outcome every single time. That gray area, it turns out, was where most of the fun lived, and I was missing out.

The summer between my freshman and sophomore years of college, I had a choice to make. Since my freshman year had been spent mostly in the bowels of depression and severe anxiety, my mental health had significantly declined, and I wasn't sure what to do. I could either apply to other schools and start anew, or I could face my fears and insecurities head-on.

I fortunately chose the latter.

My university offered upperclassmen a chance to settle in early in exchange for helping freshmen and their families with their move-in experience. I signed up and was so happy I did. Instead of being nervous, anxious, and overwhelmed, I got to calmly set up, take a breather, and get to know others in my dormitory before the madness began. On the first official day of classes, I decided to break out of my usual comfort zone, let go of my assumptions, get super uncomfortable (for me), and introduce myself to every single person on my floor.

What I never expected was to gain a sudden increase in confidence, friends, and a reputation for being the go-to person for social events around campus. Turns out many other college students are trying to reconcile who they were for whom they wanted to be, and they were finding some challenges and difficulties with that metaphorical tug-of-war.

When I gave myself permission to try new things and stop boxing myself into what I thought I was *supposed* to do, I quickly became this person who had more fun. I suddenly became more confident, someone others gravitated toward. I could be both smart and social at the same time. I didn't have to compromise or hide pieces of my personality. It was even a little exhilarating to discover that I enjoyed learning, growing, and being okay with living life in my messy middle ground. That's where everybody else was hanging out anyway.

I spoke with Dima Ghawi, the author of *Breaking Vases*, about this idea of discovery. Raised in a traditional, conservative Christian community in Jordan, she grew up believing that obeying others, especially men and her elders, was the primary way to respect her family and thus lead a meaningful, honorable life.

Her grandmother instilled this idea in her that a woman was like a vase. Her duty and responsibility was to preserve that perfect and fragile image, never to crack or be broken. She recalls her saying, "If it breaks, you can't fix it, you can't glue it back together, you have to throw it out."

Clearly, perfectionism was alive and well here, something programmed very early on, leading her to believe she couldn't make any mistakes and had to follow the rules. Sounds familiar, right?

When she accepted a marriage proposal from an older man from California, she thought she managed to flee her oppressive Middle Eastern culture. However, not too soon after she moved to the States did she discover this new life of hers was not what it initially seemed—quite the opposite, in fact. Her new husband was very controlling and traditional, exactly what she believed she had escaped.

When I asked her about this time in her life, she told me it was a harrowing one, full of fear and dark moments where she questioned everything to its core. She became depressed and didn't recognize it for a long time because she didn't understand it. Depression was never talked about openly in her culture growing up. Once she realized what was happening and that it was possible to not feel that way by changing something in her life, she then concluded that "perfectionism no longer fit in my life."

As she explained further, "Women rank themselves so low so often. There's a gap between how they see themselves and how others see them. Often, it's better than how they see themselves. The low confidence in women—we keep comparing ourselves to these perfectionist ideals. Negative stories affect us."

For Dima, those old tendencies and antiquated ways of thinking were not conducive to the new life she wanted to start living. She forged a new path for herself, a bold new identity, and discovered she had more courage than she thought. While she continues to receive death threats from her father and other family members on a regular basis, she knows it is all worth it.

Divorce is still very much a taboo subject in many Middle Eastern families, especially religious conservative ones. A 2004 study interviewing divorced Israeli women found many coped by "relying on their inner resources and the strength their children gave them, while their own families of origin were almost uniformly critical and rejecting" (Cohen and Savaya 2004). The study's title is none other than "Broken Glass," nearly identical to Dima Ghawi's memoir. It connotes this idea that a woman is without imperfections and perfectly preserved, but if tested and stressed too hard, she becomes broken and damaged, never to be repaired.

Not okay!

Fighting against this idea is a must. In some cases, it's the very difference between life and death. If we allow ourselves the chance to discover more of life, more about what we might want, more about ourselves, more about the world around us, then we may just find a different way forward. A life without mistakes, imperfections, challenges, freedoms, and experiences is just not a life.

Take it from Dima:

- Continue to question everything.
- Invest in yourself—job, education, etc.
- Be careful who you surround yourself with.

Discovery doesn't have to be scary. We don't have to push ourselves to uncomfortable places or be afraid of what we don't already know yet or overcommit to something new right away. We get to decide how we want to live our lives.

That can't be understated: We get to live our *own* lives.

Life is a constant journey of discovery. We are continuously learning, growing, and changing, whether or not we consciously notice it. If we don't like something, we have the power and permission to change it.

After all, every single one of us goes in and out of this world the same way. It's what happens in between that really matters.

E

E IS FOR EMOTIONS

Humans are naturally emotional creatures. It's how we differentiate ourselves from other mammals. These mental states play a central role in how we relate to each other and the world around us. They help shape our responses, or lack thereof, to our experiences.

But when something doesn't go perfectly for me, my emotions run a wild goose chase around my brain and sometimes my body. I become anxious, angry, and annoyed. In layman's terms, I can flip out, fly off the handle, and get really pissed off.

Why?

Well, in short, I feel shame. I get frustrated when things don't go according to plan, and I've always got the sense that for the longest time, I've lacked the tools to learn how to regulate my emotions and just calm the *F* down.

In a *Journal of Counseling Psychology* study, administrators Aldea and Rice found, "Perfectionistic individuals focus a great deal of energy on self-evaluations. They are prone to experiencing emotions such as shame, guilt, and embarrassment" (Aldea and Rice 2006, 499).

Of course. Strive for the ultimate in everything we do. If we don't achieve it, we get frustrated and feel ashamed, like we failed and it was all our fault.

Scientifically speaking, it turns out there may be a psychological tie here that we didn't account for initially: emotional dysregulation. In case you weren't familiar, this is the mismanagement or poor management of our emotions or our emotional response (Davis 2021). When emotions are not managed well, things can actively escalate or fall apart. In essence, "Perfectionism... involves a tendency to perceive and focus on failure. Individuals with maladaptive perfectionistic tendencies constantly strive for perfection, are unable to be satisfied with what ordinarily might be considered a success or superior achievement, and may show greater emotional vulnerability to daily hassles and stress..." (Aldea and Rice, 2006, 506). Taken a step further, it can also result in "nonsuicidal self-injurious behavior, suicidal ideation and attempts, excessive substance use, and impulsivity" (Rogers Behavioral Health 2023).

Sounds pretty bleak.

In college, I spent most of my time trying to control my body because I felt unable to reconcile my emotions any other way. Instead of asking for help or talking about how I felt (lost, alone, confused, scared, nervous, worried, etc.), I turned inward, destroying myself physically and emotionally. I'd lash out while drunk since that seemed to be the only time when my words and feelings flowed freely, unrestricted by fears and anxieties. Concerned family and friends tried to make me understand the damage I was inflicting. But I'd flip out, try to defend my behavior and actions, and get emotionally distraught. On and on, the cycle would go.

And here's what that can lead to: "Emotional dysregulation and defense mechanisms maintain perfectionists' negative affect and prevent them from moving beyond the distress associated with perceived stressful situations" (Aldea and Rice 2006, 506).

This makes perfect sense. I've shaken my fists, experienced body shutters, sworn out loud, made daggers with my eyes, pulled my own hair, kicked and punched inanimate objects, you name it.

At my worst, I have become unable to regulate and calm myself for days on end.

Living this way is no fun at all. It can put undue stress on an already volatile situation. The emotional weight can sometimes resemble the physical weight, pulling someone deeper into a pit of despair that seems impossible to climb out of.

Our feelings, thoughts, and emotions swirling around in our brain, telling us we're not good enough and that we need to try harder, are the very things holding us back. A perfectionist's emotions, like anxiety, shame, embarrassment, etc., are a storm cloud driving us further into a downward spiral, and round and round we go until something eventually breaks.

So if our emotions are super difficult to manage and regulate, what should we do?

Lucky for us, Dima Ghawi and Julia Gallo have some ideas.

When Dima realized her deep depression was prohibitive to her happiness, she knew she had to make some changes. In her culture, she was never taught about depression, so it took her a very long time to fully recognize what it was. Once she did, she was able to make emotional changes to help build a better life—happier, more purposeful, more confident.

At a TEDxTruro event in 2021, Julia LeGallo, a business development and marketing manager based in Cornwall, England, spoke about her life experiences with perfectionism and how she found herself one day thinking about ending her life. On the surface, people assumed she "had it all"—the house, the job, the marriage. But underneath that façade, she couldn't bear being anxious or judged or out of control any longer.

Luckily, she was able to come to a place of self-awareness that allowed her to cope in a positive way. She shares, "Cognitive behavioral therapy (CBT), which focuses on improving emotional regulation by challenging harmful beliefs and putting strategies in place to solve problems, worked wonders" (LeGallo 2021).

For those unfamiliar with the technique, CBT is used to reframe negative or compulsive thoughts as part of treatment for a variety of different disorders, such as panic disorder, OCD, general anxiety, social anxiety, post-traumatic stress, and more. As of 2013, 69 percent of the roughly 2,300 psychologists surveyed in the United States used CBT as a technique to help treat their patients (Brown 2013). For Julia, it helped her recognize that she was good enough and perfectionism was not serving her well, and it offered techniques to combat those negative emotions. We're allowed to feel and react, but not to the degree where it causes more damage than before.

Life is gray, messy, and chaotic, and we're giving it our best shot. Perfectionism is subjective, and our image of perfect may not be the same as someone else's.

Julia also mentioned two other techniques that aided in her recovery. One was breathing exercises, which reduce stress and relax the nervous system (Adele 2023). It may sound silly, but hear me out. By controlling our breathing better, we can control our body's responses better. We become more relaxed and able to have a clearer mind, which would benefit us as we come out of a downward emotional spiral, right? The second technique Julia used is bullet journaling. Different from your standard "assignment notebook," it requires task categorization and ways to measure completion. Daily, monthly, and yearly reflections play a part as well, in addition to helping you see progress and success along the way (Garrity and Schumer 2022).

I loved this comment from Julia: "Let's remove the imposed toxicity" (LeGallo 2021).

Many of us use our emotions to justify feeling like crap, like we need to be punished. But that's typical of our own doing. We impose those standards for success, those high goals, that unattainable nirvana. As a result, that toxic emotional response takes over, driving us toward fire after fire after fire. Light one and they all begin to burn.

So, how do we extinguish them?

Here's what I learned.

We need to take the time to listen to and understand our thoughts and emotions. We need to better recognize when our feelings are valid and perhaps more universal (e.g., it's natural to feel upset if you fail a test) versus when our emotions are negatively dictating how we respond to the rest of the world. If we can identify our triggers or just take a deep breath, we can change how we feel. If we can change how we feel, we might be able to change our outlook on ourselves and our lives. Getting through challenges, struggles, and tasks can be easier.

We need to stop beating ourselves up. We're often our own worst critic! When I was trying to control my body and be as thin as I could possibly get, no one said, "Wow, you need to lose more weight because I can't be friends with you otherwise." Kinda nuts when you say it out loud, right?

We impose these ridiculous and impossible standards on ourselves, only to be disappointed and ashamed when we haven't reached them. Our emotions run wild, bleeding toxicity into our bodies, making us feel lost, unmotivated, despondent, and stressed, among other things.

Instead, I propose being more empathetic and forgiving, understanding not everyone defines standards with the same scorecard or has the same expectations as we do. So let's stop comparing ourselves and just breathe.

Diaphragm in, diaphragm out. Count two, three, four, and exhale.

Ommmmm.

We can do this.

F

F IS FOR FAILURE

Failure feels like a dirty word.

Something gross, negative, nasty, threatening even, like I should avoid it at all costs.

Perfectionists spend so much time actively seeking ways to avoid failure. Anything less than winning or achieving means we have failed. An A- is mediocre. An A+ is much better.

In my case, that meant avoiding nearly all situations where I knew I wouldn't come out on top.

Take basketball, for example. I remember very vividly, as a child, I refused to play this sport. I somehow knew I wouldn't excel at it, and I loathed having to play it in gym class. I was a good runner, I could play volleyball, I could be decent enough at soccer, but for some reason basketball was not my forte.

To me, failing signified I was incapable of doing something, I didn't try hard enough, and I didn't have what it took to accomplish something. I felt it was my personal fault I couldn't excel. Like I was dumb or couldn't grasp a concept that others could. So, I never took big chances or allowed myself to make key mistakes I should have.

But why? Why would I avoid something if I don't even know what I'm getting myself into? How can I predict if I will be *good* or *bad* at something before I even start?

Best-selling author, founder, and podcast host on reinvention Roger Osorio has a term for this, and it's brilliant: *premeditated perfectionism*. He defines it as avoiding situations where we strongly assume we'll fail and thus not be perfect. It's going into situations, almost knowing the outcome, and choosing those we feel we will do amazingly—pretty great term.

As I mulled this over, I thought about all my premeditated avoidances: basketball, taking hard classes in school, calling people over the phone, asking for help, doing a backflip, choosing a challenging career path, being away from home, doing anything social, admitting being scared to speak up, running for class office, applying to selective colleges or universities, and other instances I'm sure.

I'd think, *If I could anticipate these seemingly difficult things in advance and purposefully opt out, I'd be golden.*

Or at least that's what I told myself.

Over time, I've learned everyone really does need to be given the freedom to fail. It should have a different name that doesn't sound so ominous, like "choices that didn't work out" or "oopsie moments" or something a little less tragic. Then I wouldn't feel so bad.

Rejection or failure are not bad words. These can be times to let you know how to make improvements, gain insights into something new, or learn what you do or don't like or are or are not enjoying.

At the beginning of my freshman year of college, I was all excited to meet new people, especially boys. I grew up in a somewhat small town, so I was the typical spoiled middle-class white girl. My own self-inflicted moniker. After not having a ton of luck in the boyfriend department, I thought, *Hey, now that I'm in college around new people, I bet I could find a boyfriend in no time! I'm funny, charming, smart, attractive, and have tons to offer!*

Yeah, that's right. Keep thinking those qualities aren't like 99 percent of other women out there. It's more than just the appearance and basics of someone's personality that makes a long-term relationship work. After all, there are so many songs about love and commitment that no one really has a one-size-fits-all solution. That's why it's so hard to figure out. Relationships are not about what works on paper.

I wish I could have realized that sooner, but hey, I was only seventeen. Still young, still growing, and still not fully sure of myself.

That fall, during the first few months of college, I met a guy. We hit it off, and then I started asking what was wrong with me to make him not want to be in a relationship. He responded with an answer mirroring many new college freshman guys, "I just don't want a relationship right now."

I took that to mean: "You're not what I'm looking for. You should probably change something about yourself because I'm just not that into you. In other words, Vanessa, you are not girlfriend worthy. You suck. You're a failure."

I can see how woefully wrong and immature that mindset is now. At the time, I heard his words and translated them into perfectionist failure speak: "You wanted to be boyfriend and girlfriend, and he doesn't want to be, so therefore, something is wrong with you. You are inadequate by his standards, so, in conclusion, you are not worthy of being loved. Not now, maybe not ever."

It is nuts to think I once considered my reactionary assumptions normal.

But with love and relationships in general, it's tough to pinpoint and make sense of it all. There isn't a set rubric to grade a relationship on the same scale. Many people consider something wrong with them until they meet someone who makes them feel different, safe, and accepted for who they are, no matter what side they show. So cliché, so old school, but oh so true.

Putting yourself out there is hard. Letting everyone get to know the *real you* is just plain difficult. Humans are multilayered, complex, and tough to simplify. More often than not, we only show the world partial sections of ourselves. Having someone else love and accept every part of you, from headcase to toe, is an enormous and chancy undertaking. Sharing our innermost ideas and stories, the thoughts inside our heads, make us scared. Vulnerability can be, and for perfectionists is, very intimidating. And for so many years, I equated vulnerability with a high chance of failure because if I exposed the parts of me I was still unsure about or not confident in, I could get hurt or judged—my nightmare.

I spoke with life coach Keri Martinez about failure, and she shared something I had never considered. To her, success and failure are often tied together because "failure and success are two sides of the same coin." You can't have one without the other. If we don't fail, then we can't learn. If we can't learn, we'll never grow. If we never grow, we'll never succeed. Success, by definition, is needing to figure out what doesn't work to know what does.

In other words, the very nature of this term is simply because of what it is not.

Say that again—success is defined because of what it is not. The journey to finding out the way forward (sometimes a painful, embarrassing, frustrating process) is a necessary step to achieving success.

I appreciated her comments on this because sometimes it seems hard not to get boxed into thinking failure is almost always a bad thing. Even saying the word aloud makes me cringe. Failure. Ew. Ugh.

Showing our humanity and vulnerability through our failures doesn't make us weak. It can make us stronger and take us to new depths and heights than we thought possible. If we take steps to examine, assess and attempt to fix and improve, then we can grow and learn, perhaps shape ourselves into something different.

In her revolutionary book, *Mindset*, Dr. Carol Dweck goes into painstaking detail explaining the difference between the growth and fixed mindsets of individuals. With regards to failure, having a fixed mindset can be quite detrimental and paralyzing. We become unmotivated, despondent, and wallow in our shortcomings, not focused on anything but the negative effects of what we've done or didn't do. As for the growth mindset, well, that's a much more positive outlook and response to failure. "Even in the growth mindset, failure can be a painful experience. But it doesn't define you. It's a problem to be faced, dealt with, and learned from" (Dweck 2006, 33). Instead of relating to failure in a fixed, negative way, associated with feelings of less-than, unworthiness, ineptitude, and inability, one can view them as "motivating. They're informative. They're a wake-up call" (Dweck 2006, 99).

Failure to me today means I'm operating on a gradient, where everything is more relative and gray than black and white and exactly yes or no. And I'm learning. Maybe that's what the new word is—learn. Failing makes us think there's an endpoint. There's something to be ashamed of and embarrassed about, even feared. Instead, I'd rather look at these shortcomings as opportunities to grow, develop, and improve. We should embrace the freedom to fail.

To experience success, you gotta flip that coin over and recognize failure for what it really is—a teachable moment.

G
G IS FOR GOALS

To be human is to have goals. It's what separates us from most other species.

We like to focus our attention and brain power on not just the essentials (food, water, housing, etc.) but ideas about a future or desired result that we want to achieve.

But what happens when those dreams are too big?

According to the *Harvard Business Review*, "As high achievers, we're programmed to 'go big or go home' and to 'set big hairy audacious goals.' Big goals are more burdensome than motivational. They require daunting effort to accomplish and sustain in our busy lives. Falling short of a lofty goal creates a negative spiral of discouragement, deterring future action. Instead of striding forward, we slide backward" (Nawaz 2020).

We look at them like they are these huge mountainous hurdles that get us scared and want to run in the other direction. They are obstacles when they should be paths without barriers. Somehow, we need to break ourselves from this idea.

But how?

In the summer of 2022, I met two keynote speakers at a work conference out in San Francisco, *New York Times* best-selling author and career and workplace expert Lindsey Pollak and entrepreneur, author, and Georgetown Professor Eric Koester. I have attended quite a few conferences in my time, but never have I felt like I was at the exact place I needed to be than during those few days in August. Other than my wedding and the births of my sons, of course.

Lindsey spoke about some themes present in her book, *Recalculating.* As a career expert, she understood many of the challenges that higher education leaders, our conference attendees, were faced with—how to engage their students and alumni in meaningful ways that could contribute positively to their professional journeys.

As COVID-19 hit, she found herself having to reenvision what her career would look like when she couldn't travel and perform speaking functions. She thought about returning to her writing roots and began work on this next book. What she found through additional research was that so many of us in our careers will have to recalculate and figure out a new path based on where we find ourselves in that moment. The labor market, and subsequently the roles and skills required to keep up with it, is changing, and we need to adapt and go along for the ride (Pollack 2021).

Recalculate or perish.

So many are making pivots in their careers. A 2021 CNBC article cited that as many as four million Americans are quitting their jobs each month. The Great Resignation is indeed upon us, and it doesn't look like it's slowing down anytime soon. "Of the roughly 50 percent of employed Americans who intend to make career changes because of the COVID-19 pandemic, 41 percent are seeking flexible or remote work, 39 percent desire a raise or promotion, and 33 percent are interested in changing industries" (Hess 2021). Employees no longer stay at one company for the duration of their professional life. They will almost certainly have more than one stop along the way.

I'm a good example. I started out in educational travel sales, then transitioned into higher education, specifically admissions, then shifted over to enrollment management before diving back into the corporate world, this time in EdTech. While education was a common thread throughout, each of these journeys were unique and a recalculation.

I have been laid off twice, and each time I had to figure out what was next for me—pretty immediately too. After all, I had bills to pay and a career to get after, and the second time I had my family to help support, so the stakes were even higher.

Being laid off is tough. It's never a welcomed situation. Even if you expect it and can see it coming, it doesn't make you feel any better. This can also be a perfectionist's worst nightmare. If your job is a big part of who you are, it can seem like a huge blow to your identity. All that hard work, all that effort each and every day, all that striving and getting after it, was all for nothing. They decided they didn't need you anymore, and that sucks.

So, what does all this have to do with goals?

Well, everything.

Goals keep us motivated, but unattainable ones can arrest us in place, slowing us down and preventing us from moving on. When I walked up to Lindsey after her keynote that day at the conference, she said essentially the same thing. I mentioned I had been trying to write for years and get published but was struggling to envision how to get there so quickly.

Her response stuck with me. "I'm so happy to hear that! But remember, it took me twenty years to get there. It's a work in progress like everything else, and it takes time. It doesn't happen overnight."

That hit me like a dart. Small goals were really the key to achieving bigger things. From Lindsey's research, she realized recalculating requires us to be flexible in the job market and also in life. She understood change and big goals can be overwhelming, especially when we think of making big shifts, like changing career paths for example. A daunting task like that needs to be broken down in simpler terms. When we create small goals for ourselves that are more manageable and within reach, we feel more confident and are likely to succeed. The impossible suddenly becomes possible.

She used a personal example of hers to drive this point home. During the pandemic, she found herself eating way too many peanut M&Ms. To try and break this habit, she thought about stopping cold turkey but found it too difficult to stick to her end goal. Instead, she subtracted just one peanut M&M from her daily stash and kept eliminating it day by day. Having that big goal portioned into smaller, more achievable goals worked wonders!

And for the record—she still eats them, just not in such high quantities.

In addition to breaking up goals into incremental ones, there are other effective strategies we could use.

According to a 2015 study, there is empirical evidence that writing down your goals and even sharing them with others like friends, family, or colleagues makes you more likely to complete them (Gardner and Albee 2015). Accountability, commitment, and the simple act of writing goals down are successful ways to ensure completion.

What can we learn from all this?

Given that most perfectionists, if not all, create extraordinarily momentous goals for themselves because we simply must achieve more, more, more, it's no wonder we are driven to complete them with a sense of urgency. That same feeling of trying to accomplish them quickly can be intimidating. Going zero to sixty is super tough, especially if your goal is something like "Become a published author tomorrow." Well, if you haven't even written a draft, how the heck is that going to happen?

Goals can make us overwhelmed and anxious if we think about how much work we need to accomplish in just one or two steps. That might prevent us from doing anything altogether. A sense of arrested development occurs—never truly moving ahead, only stuck in place.

I know I felt this way when I was laid off. I had high goals and hopes and felt like, suddenly, the rug was ripped out from underneath me. I felt disoriented and confused, not knowing where to start over again. I had no clue how to get a new job so quickly because that's what I thought—it had to be immediate. Otherwise, it was my fault.

But, like most things in life, big goals take time.

If we take just one small step at a time, it makes us feel more accomplished and confident and motivated to keep moving. How often do you put things you've already done on a checklist for the day? I know I do. Suddenly I feel better, like I was productive, that I put some meaningful energy out into the world, and I can then find the strength to keep on trucking.

Our intention of a goal is to complete the goal. So let's stop putting up barriers and ballooning them until they inevitably pop. Start small, win big. Penny in, dollar out. We got this!

H

H IS FOR HOPE

Hope is a hard concept for perfectionists to grasp, yet we cling to it with such vigor, tightening our grip on it at every moment. It's an intangible feeling that gives us reason to believe things might actually work out. It drives us forward, pushing us to keep going, keep thinking, and wish for the best.

But what if we're always thinking the worst? What if hope is just a placeholder to make us briefly feel better about situations where we know we don't have control?

I'd hazard a guess that many of you reading this feel the same way. Hope is just a feeling that we can control, but we cannot control the outcome of a particular event or situation. That sucks, but latching on to hope as a safety net is sometimes all we have to rely on.

The year 2020 was unlike any other in living memory. Other than the 1918 Spanish flu pandemic, humanity had never previously seen something so pervasive, so tragic, so ugly, so unnerving. It was the ultimate showdown of good versus evil in ways billions of us never expected. Aside from the usual news stories, we were introduced to a new deadly disease, COVID-19—one that swept the globe quicker than a sneeze and with a force no one ever expected.

We became prisoners within our own homes and fearful of the very air we breathed. We practiced social distancing from colleagues, friends, family, and, in many ways, both physical and emotional, from ourselves. Suffering and sadness were running rampant. Mental health isn't just a bougie term anymore. Nothing is or feels remotely *normal*, and there seems to be no end in sight.

When this first happened, I was not only terrified, but I was left feeling hopeless. At a time when everyone, not just perfectionists, needed hope that this disease would wage its war quickly and mildly, we were all left dumbfounded. Not even the most optimistic people could fathom a near future that wasn't despondent, tragic, or horrific. Life became a series of events from the movie *Contagion*, where everyone suffers, and humanity is left crumbling into rubble.

Even in year two, things didn't improve. In fact, they steadily got worse. According to Gallup's Negative Experience Index, "In 2021, four in ten adults worldwide said they experienced a lot of worry (42 percent) or stress (41 percent), and slightly more than three in ten experienced a lot of physical pain (31 percent). More than one in four experienced sadness (28 percent), and slightly fewer experienced anger (23 percent)" (Ray 2022).

These are findings across the board, so you can imagine that for perfectionists, these statistics would be even higher and, thus, worse. Typically, we collapse in these conditions, crumbling and crashing, burning hard and coming away scathed, scarred, and, you could say, scared.

How would we get by? What would provide comfort or some semblance of normalcy?

I'll be honest here—this was and, to some degree, still is me. To be a perfectionist in these times was downright awful. Moments of crying, worrying, and stressing every time I heard a cough or felt off, trying desperately to control everything and everyone around me when that is nearly impossible, figuring out how to work and take care of my then eight-month-old all at the same time, and just generally seeing the world go to hell. These all kept me up at night and sucked any remaining energy reserves I had.

However, here's my thought if anything positive came out of COVID-19. In the darkest of times, when we feel like giving up the idea that things will get better, when all our energy is beyond spent, and when we have struggled so hard to keep it all together, there is still one more option: hope.

Hope that things will one day be manageable, or at the very least tolerable, once again.

Hope that we will go back to work and school and play without being fearful of opening our airways to breathe without a mask or sanitizing everything in sight.

Hope that we can repair the social, mental, and physical connections that were lost, ones we thought were dead or extinct.

Hope that this can't be the end for all of us, the world, and humanity.

For me personally, I find it very difficult to consistently think in this way. I am not what you would call a Positive Polly or a wishful thinker. I am someone who freaks out, overthinks, and spirals downward—fast. I make choices based not on reasonable thinking sometimes but on imagining every possible negative and tragic outcome. When faced with the possibility of failure, even if I think I catch a whiff of it, I avoid it. Detour! Detour! Detour! Go with what you know will work out. That's the safest.

Well, unfortunately, 2020 gave birth to a very different world, one that has quite literally become the epitome of anti-perfectionism. So many unknowns, so many challenges, so many fears, so many failures, and so many reasons to doubt and lose ourselves in a dark haze of stormy and terrible thoughts. So many... imperfections.

It's easy to keep thinking this way. Spiraling is natural—literally. The shape connotes going around in circles, seemingly without end. But if I really want to keep going, if I have any chance of making it out of the aftermath of 2020 alive and intact, then I have to approach life with hope. I must realter my mindset and try my hardest to believe something must give. Something must work out, something good must happen.

There almost wasn't any other choice. Because the alternative would be to keep suffering and let my mental insanity and running script of negativity and fear own the rest of my life.

The truth is, good things are happening. We just may have to work harder to focus and find them.

Personally,

I am still healthy.

I am still employed.

I am still married.

I am still a mother.

I am still loved.

I am still here.

Hope is tough to grasp as it's intangible but still within our control to feel and own. It can teach us to lean into our emotions and our feelings and believe that sometimes it's okay if every scenario isn't tailor-made to our specifications. It can also draw attention to the positive things and can serve as motivation to keep going, even if we don't have it all figured out, planned, or executed.

I know plenty of people are living, maybe not thriving but surviving—still fighting and working hard. Being human means being able to share stories, communicate, and commiserate to find common ground and understanding. Hope is one of those ideas we can and should rally around. More than ever, we need hope to cure these diseases and embrace the unknown.

I
I IS FOR IMPOSTOR SYNDROME

I can't think of a moment in my life when imposter syndrome didn't make an appearance.

In third grade, I didn't feel as smart as my fellow students, and I thought the only reason I went on to the next grade was because of pure dumb luck or some other error.

In ninth grade, I vividly recall my math teacher saying that no one had ever managed to move up a level and get straight A's. It was next to impossible. And for the record, I did it. I got all A's the next year at a higher math level. And while I felt proud of that accomplishment, I also believed I wasn't as intelligent as my peers. I thought I was just decent at memorizing stuff.

In college, it was less about academics and more outward appearance related. I never felt like one of the cool kids. I was always the outsider looking in, and when I did go to parties, I often felt like the wolf in sheep's clothing, impersonating another version of myself, like I had to *turn on* a different button that magically turned the regular me into a naturally social, party-going version of me.

Early in my career, hitting my sales goals even felt like a lie. Why was I making and exceeding quota? I wasn't a *real* salesperson, right?

First coined in the 1970s, impostor syndrome "occurs among high achievers who are unable to internalize and accept their success. They often attribute their accomplishments to luck rather than to ability, and fear that others will eventually unmask them as a fraud" (Weir 2013).

Especially in the workplace, it's becoming more prevalent. For females in particular, as much as 75 percent of female executives have experienced impostor syndrome, and 53 percent of female professionals aged twenty-five to thirty-four are currently experiencing it (Nicols 2020).

As a working mom of two young boys, I still have moments when I feel I'm not good enough and just passing through by the skin of my teeth. Especially when it comes to motherhood, sometimes I get the sense that everyone else was born for this role, and I'm barely masquerading in it. Perfect moms have it all together and do everything correctly, right?

Those of us who suffer from constant impostor syndrome always feel like we are less than, that we won't make the grade, and that we can't possibly be an expert at something.

And yet, there's usually no proof or evidence to support feeling this way. This robs us of being able to take credit for the hard work we've actually done. It can destroy our confidence and ability to achieve success in something we should be confident in.

We fear someone is going to shout, "They're an impostor! They have no idea what they're talking about! They're a liar!"

What we hear is: *I am not an expert, I am not smart, I am not worthy.*

Even celebrities, who seem to have it all, experience impostor syndrome: Lady Gaga, Serena Williams, Sheryl Sandberg, Tina Fey, Maya Angelou, David Bowie, Arianna Huffington, Tom Hanks, and the list goes on and on. Sheryl Sandberg didn't think she deserved to be at Harvard, and even decades after her success, she felt "there are still days when I wake up feeling like a fraud, not sure I should be where I am" (Leadem 2017). Even as a Nobel Laureate, Maya Angelou questioned her writing abilities: "I have written eleven books, but each time I think, 'uh oh, they're going to find out now. I've run a game on everybody, and they're going to find me out" (Warrell 2014).

In 2018, former First Lady Michelle Obama spoke to an all-girls school in London as part of her book tour. Although she is widely recognized as an inspiration to so many, she still finds herself having "a little [bit of] impostor syndrome, it never goes away, that you're actually listening to me. It doesn't go away, that feeling that you shouldn't take me that seriously. What do I know? I share that with you because we all have doubts in our abilities, about our power and what that power is" (BBC News 2018). Despite her achievements, Michelle Obama still had moments when she questioned herself and her capability to share her very valid knowledge and expertise.

Pop icon and fashion entrepreneur Jessica Simpson constantly suffered from these insecurities, sometimes impeding her from moving on and doing what came naturally to her.

Before she reached sky-high levels of fame, she felt pressured to be a certain version of herself that would please others, not truly feeling that her authentic self was good enough. She gets very candid and honest in her memoir, *Open Book*: "I was working so hard to be a rigid version of *godly* that I judged so many people. I held myself to an insane standard, and while I beat myself up about always falling short, I definitely held it against the people who I thought weren't trying" (Simpson 2020, 92). Ultimately, she was hurting herself more than anyone else by trying to morph into whatever she perceived others wanted.

Ironically, losing your sense of self by trying to be someone you are not can feed the flames of impostor syndrome.

According to an article written by a self-identifying impostor in the medical field, Sumina Mainali writes, "Negative thinking, self-doubt, and self-sabotaging one's own successes are characteristic behaviors of those suffering from impostor syndrome. They often attribute any success they have achieved to luck or perfect timing. Feelings of low self-esteem and lack of confidence are also common. They live in fear that they won't live up to expectations and will ultimately be exposed as a fraud. Impostors set very challenging goals and feel disappointed when they fall short" (Mainali 2020).

If impostor syndrome is tied to feelings of worthiness or lack thereof, what should we do?

When I interviewed Unstoppable Latina CEO Paulette Piñero for this book, she gave me an utterly simple yet brilliant recommendation: take ridiculously small steps.

As an entrepreneur hoping to inspire other female Latinx leaders, she knows a thing or two about business, management, client relations, marketing, and branding. Yet impostor syndrome was tied strongly to inadequacy (a.k.a. worthiness). If she failed, it would be the end of the world. Everyone would find out she was a fraud, her career and life would be over, and that would be it. Conflict and failure were not options. Over time, she observed that while she was experiencing impostor syndrome, it felt as if her "body [stopped] ongoing action on things that [I'm] best positioned to do."

I loved how she described this sensation, and it's true. It's like we are being riveted in place, prevented from moving ahead, like the inertia that should naturally propel us forward is being stopped by an invisible force.

Over time, she realized the expectations of others were holding her back from doing what felt natural for her—leading. She knew she excelled at certain things, so why would she continue to doubt those instincts?

For Jessica Simpson, realizing there was a bigger force at play made all the difference: "My purpose, however, is bigger than my fear of judgment" (Simpson 2020, 8). Her unwavering faith gave her the power to stand alone and write this very difficult memoir of her life. There are so many challenges, mistakes, and heartbreak, but all worth telling to an audience who may also suffer from the same problems and experiences.

And finally, Michelle Obama has some suggestions: "My advice to young women is that you have to start by getting those demons out of your head. The questions I ask myself—'Am I good enough?'—that haunts us because the messages that are sent from the time we are little is: maybe you are not, don't reach too high, don't talk too loud" (BBC News 2018).

We must put those demons to rest and stop believing there is any genuine evidence to support feeling like an impostor. And so, while we may not be able to avoid times when those sentiments surface, we can certainly treat it like an unwelcomed friend. Tell it to get the hell outta here!

J
J IS FOR JOB

I'm curious. How do you normally introduce yourself at social events?

It could be a work function, a networking event, a conference, a party where maybe you only know some individuals, or really anything.

If I were a betting woman, I'd put some serious money on the fact your answer would be your job. The role you perform most days of the week, whether a full-time employee, parent, student, or whatever else occupies the majority of your time, is likely how most of us quantify who we are. At least in the Western World, it might go something like this: "Hi, I'm Vanessa, I'm an insert-your-position-here. What do you do?" It's a core part of our identity.

For perfectionists, our jobs are more than just conversation accoutrements. They're the main meal. After all, who are we without a purpose? Jobs showcase our worthiness as a person, and if we don't have a job, we aren't as worthy.

This is super problematic, of course.

But if that wasn't bad enough, we like to pile on more stress. Outdoing ourselves, competing to reach the top, attempting to be the best at every turn—it's exhausting.

According to a 2018 *Harvard Business Review* article, "Perfectionists strive to produce flawless work, and they also have higher levels of motivation and conscientiousness than nonperfectionists. However, they are also more likely to set inflexible and excessively high standards, to evaluate their behavior overly critically, to hold an all-or-nothing mindset about their performance, and to believe their self-worth is contingent on performing perfectly. Studies have also found that perfectionists have higher levels of stress, burnout, and anxiety" (Swider 2021).

Doesn't that sound delightful?

It seems that perfectionism can toe the line between being helpful and detrimental. Well, is it really an asset or a weakness in the workplace? Which one seems to be more prevalent, and what does it mean?

In that same *Harvard Business Review* article, a meta-study conducted from the 1980s to today that examined almost 25,000 working-age subjects had some interesting results. While the individuals' motivation and adherence to producing excellence were generally viewed as positive outcomes, they also suffered from burnout and were more likely to have negative health consequences, such as anxiety, stress, and depression. Said another way: "If perfectionism is expected to impact employee performance by increased engagement and motivation, then that impact is being offset by opposing forces, like higher depression and anxiety, which have serious consequences beyond just the workplace" (Swider 2021).

Okay, that is depressing.

But it can also be liberating.

From that research alone, we can conclude that perfectionism doesn't seem to make a big difference when it comes to producing high-quality work. It may serve as a motivator and help us get closer to our goals, but it could also be a barrier to accomplishment and just *getting it done*. Maybe good work can be good enough.

Life coach Keri Martinez knows all too well about this phenomenon. Growing up in the Church of Latter-Day Saints, Keri was conditioned to believe certain ways of thinking about herself and the world around her. Once she realized there were other perspectives out there, her mindset shifted.

Now, as a life coach and motivational speaker, she helps others figure out their next steps, especially when it comes to their careers. She compiled a list of lies of perfectionism, and her first point is spot on here: "Your worth as a person comes from the work you produce."

She argues that this lie causes us to falsely believe nothing will ever be good enough, and that can result in half-finished work, nothing at all produced, or just torturing ourselves repeatedly with draft after draft, a vicious cycle.

I must admit, I spent most of my life firmly believing this.

Throughout my professional career, there were definitely moments where I was sincerely convinced my worth as a person came from what I was able to achieve and contribute to the team and the company.

It wasn't until I had my first child and became a mother that I truly realized my value reached far beyond the workplace. I believed I was worth significantly more than what I accomplished or didn't at the office. Instead of my job being the primary way I defined myself, it was only part of the equation.

In the "Anxious Achiever" podcast hosted by Morra Aarons-Mele, she interviews Dr. Thomas Greenspon, who has written a book or two about perfectionists. Within the workplace, he shares there are three qualities that don't actually depend on perfectionism: "talent, energy, and commitment. Those three things, if you took away perfectionism, would not change" (Aarons-Mele 2022).

I'm sorry, what?

The irony, of course, is that the struggle is not necessary and, most times, is superfluous. The push and drive to be perfect does not serve anyone, least of all the perfectionists themselves.

Kinda makes me wish I had learned this a lot sooner.

But beyond jobs tied to worth and talent, many people are convinced there is a *perfect* job out there—but why? What does that even mean?

And why are we seemingly jealous of others when we think they "have it"?

As *New York Times* best-selling author and workplace expert Lindsey Pollak says, "Envy doesn't have to be a negative emotion. It can be a catalyst. Inspiration and extraordinarily detailed advice are always a click away. While aimlessly scrolling through social media can be toxic and addictive, actively using it for research is a remarkably effective way to learn from successful people" (Pollak 2021, 29). In other words, do the work to get to better work—get curious, research, evaluate, and have some conversations.

Gather that info like the perfectionist you are and turn it into your new superpower!

Perfectionism can make us believe the unattainable perfect job does exist and that our work is tied to our worth as human beings. But, more often than not, it creates negative feelings associated with not being good enough, not getting anywhere, and not being the best.

So, turn those emotions into positive ones. Use them as motivation to assess what's truly important. Take the time to evaluate what's meaningful to you outside of the job itself: it might be spending time with family, having flexible work hours, the chance to travel, or the opportunity to pursue a passion project.

Good can be good enough, remember? Then you can enjoy other parts of your life because they do exist.

K

K IS FOR KIDS

Remember that story from the introduction—my first day of third grade when the bus was late?

Well, it seems that perfectionism existed even back then, so early on in my childhood.

Why is that? How does it start?

It turns out not only are we partly born with it (think: genetics and inherited traits), but we are often heavily shaped by our environment. This can include overbearing and critical caregivers, a turbulent upbringing, pressure from the community or peers, as well as exposure to a slew of mental health issues (BetterUp 2022).

The classic nature versus nurture argument.

In my case, my parents were in no way super overbearing or highly critical of me. In fact, they were quite the opposite. They reminded me to try as best I could and that good could be good enough. It would be fine if I was a C student. A's were not necessary to them. Earning a C could mean I gave it my best effort, which was all that mattered.

So why didn't I listen? And how did I end up this way?

When some of my high school peers found out I was writing a book about perfectionism, nearly all of them were like, "Oh yes, classic!" We grew up in this secluded, privileged bubble and were taught we had to, at any cost, outperform, overdeliver, and overachieve. I attended the top-ranked high school in the Boston MetroWest area, so it probably comes as no surprise that my cultural surroundings (community, peers, school) had a lot to do with fanning the flames of my perfectionist tendencies.

According to an article on Parents.com, "Extreme perfectionists often struggle with low self-esteem, are easily embarrassed, and may obsess about every mistake, real or perceived. They're the kids who become so agitated about coloring outside the lines that they'll repeatedly crumple up their paper and start over. If they answer nine out of ten questions correctly on a quiz, they'll focus on the one wrong answer rather than take pride in the right ones. They'll quit a sports team if they think they're not as good as everyone else. Even though they want to do well in school, they may procrastinate because if they don't start an assignment, they won't risk failing. They can take hours to write a three-line letter because they're so anxious about getting the wording right" (Waldman 2022).

This was me to a *T*.

I was scared to be myself, thought everything was my fault, and was easily embarrassed. I was clearly afraid and anxious, more than the average kid. It affected my social skills for several years, and I was nervous about being wrong because I didn't want to feel less than at all costs, especially in front of my peers.

If you recall from earlier, it has been said that "Perfectionism in children and teens has increased by 33 percent over the last three decades" (Newport Academy 2022). This is a scary statistic, especially in a world that is becoming overcrowded and noisy with too many people and too many high expectations.

Add on top of that the collapse of time itself—news cycles are twenty-four hours a day, we stream anything we want anytime we want, and we have instant access to just about whatever our hearts desire. We are no longer constricted by time or space at rates never seen before.

As a mom, I can say this is one of my biggest fears. I worry my rigid tendencies will seep into my parenting style. I worry my kids will learn mistakes are unacceptable, that feeling shame and doubt is normal and encouraged, and that I expect nothing but flawlessness. I fear they will grow up believing they can't fully embrace who they are and that parts of their personalities need to hide behind a mask.

I know I need to dedicate more effort to shifting these tendencies so as not to create a culture of fear. But how can I embrace the classic perfectionist I am and yet modify my behaviors to encourage my children positively?

During one of her TEDx Talks, Brené Brown mentions every single one of us is initially "hardwired for struggle when [we] get here. Our job is to look and say, you know what, you're imperfect and you're wired for struggle, but you are worthy of love and belonging" (Brown 2010).

I could not have said it better myself.

Babies enter this world crying, requiring food and comfort, and to be cared for twenty-four seven. Our job as parents needs to go beyond those basic needs.

Visibility is key. This means making sure our kids know we are here, we are present, and we love them, no matter what.

If you are a parent and wondering how to best support your child who might already be displaying inclinations toward perfectionism, there is hope. It starts with acknowledging the critical voices they have. Empathy, teaching and learning together, sharing positive statements, and modeling self-acceptance are just some of the ways we can help prevent it or at least stop it from getting worse (Waldman 2022).

These are good tips for all of us.

Former First Lady Michelle Obama believes part of the solution lies in a strong emotional education. "She instilled messages of competency, character, and worth in Malia and Sasha through what she preached and what they practiced. They needed the tools to survive the world without her" (Little 2022). In other words, ensuring her daughters felt supported, loved, and able to succeed was extremely important in helping them be comfortable and confident on their own. As parents, we always want to help and do things for our children, but we don't want to over-enable, which risks them not learning how to feel capable and strong and independent, all valuable and necessary skills in this harsh world.

It wasn't until I thought seriously about having kids that I came to terms with the negative side effects and consequences of trying to be perfect. This, of course, came with time, (re)learning and speaking to many individuals who were feeling the same way, and discussing how to best move forward. But beyond that, my future kids were my main reason for getting the help I needed to become whole again in a positive, healthy way. It was no longer only about me. It was about them. I wasn't about to risk their bright future just for my own selfish, mostly vain reasons.

Life coach Flame Schoeder says, "The very antidote to perfectionism is truth." Now, wait a minute. That sounds bizarre and frighteningly simple. Truth is the way out?

She strongly believes so. In fact, she teaches this to her clients. We can recognize the fight-or-flight instinct and reframe it. Truth helps us have more mental clarity by not succumbing to judgment or outside interpretation, and it means we're doing something that matters—seeking the truth. It can literally set us free.

During our conversation, she taught me the meaning of the word *coach* comes from the Austro-Hungarian word *kocsi*, meaning a stagecoach that transports one thing to another. It has now morphed into a term that refers to a person who brings someone from one stage (of life, of thinking, etc.) to another.

How amazing is that?

So, let's embody that mentality and be our own coach for our kids. Let's be open to making mistakes, getting messy, and being supportive of the journey rather than solely focusing on the destination. Let's be the vehicle that drives our kids forward in a healthy way rather than set unrealistic drive times.

After all, humans aren't Google Maps. We're more sophisticated than that. There have been plenty of instances where I knew a better route than what it robotically recommended.

Trust your gut and allow yourself and your kids some space to grow.

L

L IS FOR LOVE

If love is all you need, then perfectionists would be screwed.

Many of us believe love is tied to worth, and if we're not loved, then we're not worth it.

As a best-selling author, ghostwriter, and publishing consultant, Peter Economy writes, "When validation from others is needed for you to feel good... you decrease the importance of validation you could be receiving from yourself. When you depend on the opinions of others more than your own thoughts, you think of yourself as the lesser, as the person with reduced value" (Economy 2020).

Super sad, right?

So why do we seek validation through others' approval? Why can't we trust our own thoughts, judgment, decisions, expectations, etc.? When it comes to matters of the heart, why do we believe everyone else has it all figured out, and we're the ones who have it wrong?

Growing up, I never felt I was normal. I never seemed to look quite like the other girls in my grade, and I never seemed as lucky or confident. I didn't think twice about offering myself up as the metaphorical, sometimes literal, punching bag. I made fun of myself. I pretended to like certain songs or bands I didn't even know existed. I laughed at jokes when I didn't understand the punchline. At the end of the day, it was more important for me to be accepted and loved than it was to stay true to myself. I didn't mind that I compromised my intelligence, my values, and my general worth as a human being, all so I could call them my friends and feel like part of the gang. And if I wasn't gaining the official acceptance of everyone else, how could I love myself?

In college, I remember a particular instance when this whole self-unlove thing skyrocketed.

It involved a boy, and I naïvely thought I had to put up a front to impress him. He was one of the first guys I met in college who I was immediately attracted to. He was handsome, confident, dressed well, and had these piercing blue eyes and ruffled brown hair that drew me to him. I always thought guys like him were out of my league, but it turned out he was equally as attracted to and interested in me.

Holy crap, I thought. *It's actually happening!*

When he asked me to dinner, I was floored. I panicked. How was I going to show him I was girlfriend worthy? Because that's where my mind went. I didn't want to say anything that made me appear dumb, but I didn't want to sound too smart. I tried to be coy and cute, flirty and sexy, but all those things did not feel like me. I was trying to negotiate around what I thought he wanted in a girl.

I was in virgin territory here.

Dinner went well, surprisingly. Then, I heard he was planning on asking me to their spring formal dance, and I was freaking out about it. I never participated in Greek life on campus, so I didn't understand for a fraternity brother to ask someone who wasn't in a sorority to their biggest dance of the season was a huge deal. A friend told me it went against the norm and wasn't usually encouraged, so of course I felt immense pressure to put on the perfect display.

Cue the anxiety.

Long story short, I tried to become someone I didn't recognize, someone I was convinced he wanted, and it completely backfired. I dressed and spoke and acted how I envisioned a perfect sorority girl would. What does that even mean, by the way? Except, I couldn't control my true feelings when I got blackout drunk too early in the evening. I couldn't even recall the damage that was done that night. Luckily, no one was hurt, except for probably me and my pride and perhaps any possible dating future I had with this guy.

I failed to consider one of the oldest tales of time. Perhaps he was interested in me because of who I really was on the inside rather than what I was fake presenting on the outside.

As embarrassed and as mortified as I felt at that moment, I know I'm not the first or last person to do this—create a whole new personality and version of myself because I'm trying to compensate for the real me. All around the globe, people suffer from this distorted view that our worth is tied to others' opinions of us.

Celebrity and pop star Jessica Simpson writes in her 2020 memoir, *Open Book,* about being publicly and very harshly judged on the failure of her first marriage and how that affected her self-worth and trusting her own judgment when it came to finding love again. Having the public and the paparazzi scrutinizing her every move, she found it very difficult to navigate new relationships. Doubt became commonplace, and low self-esteem ensued. She sought refuge in alcohol and sex, and before long she felt lost and alone.

According to the National Organization for Women, the female sex is particularly susceptible to believing their looks are the ticket to friendships and love, with about 59 percent of girls and 63 percent of women in their sixties reporting dissatisfaction with their body shape (National Organization for Women 2014).

And it gets worse.

In April 2022, the Aesthetic Society released a press release on their annual findings on plastic surgery procedures from 2021. What they found is troubling. "The data showcases a significant increase for face, breast, and body procedures... These marked increases saw Americans spending over 14.6 billion dollars on aesthetic procedures in 2021" (Aesthetic Society 2022).

What does this all mean?

If perfectionism is defined as an "improper cognitive manipulation of the ideal self" (Fang and Liu 2022), and we're trying to morph into this unattainable, seemingly perfect version of ourselves that just doesn't exist, then we must shift that perception. If we want love in our lives for ourselves and with others, then something has to change.

We must learn how to love ourselves despite maybe feeling angry, frustrated, or despondent. We have to question the thoughts that seem unhelpful, distorted, or just downright untrue. We have to learn it's okay not to have to morph into different versions of who we naturally are.

Remember Julia LeGallo from the E is for Emotions chapter?

She shared that CBT, or cognitive behavior therapy, is one of the techniques she found instrumental in her efforts to better manage her uncontrollable and oftentimes distorted negative thoughts (LeGallo 2021). Through this version of therapy, she was able to become more self-aware in a healthy, productive way. She realized she could learn to shift her mindset in ways that would be constructive instead of destructive. With regard to self-love, this is an important lesson to learn.

Ever heard of Glennon Doyle? She is quite a formidable woman.

From a religious upbringing to becoming a bulimic alcoholic in college, to a marriage that failed under the pressure of so many expectations, denials, and trauma, to rising again as a queer woman and marrying the love of her life, she is someone to admire. After hearing many colleagues and friends mention her, I decided to find out what all the fuss was about.

They were not wrong. She did not disappoint.

Best-selling author and podcast host, Doyle is known for her musings on relationships and putting in the hard work to better understand ourselves. In her podcast series, *We Can Do Hard Things*, there's an episode ("Eff Perfection") where she deliberates on the difference between acceptance and love. Not all acceptance is love, and not all love is acceptance. You can sometimes have both in the same instance, but not always. They should not be confused as being mutually inclusive. "Love does not seek to control or change someone's humanity. If you do not fully accept who you are... you by default are not choosing love... it's acceptance" (Doyle 2021). She goes on to say you can't love someone if you can't see them. Being you, at the truest and fullest version, is the best way to get both acceptance and love.

Some real hard stuff here. It makes my brain hurt.

My Paralympian friend Monica Quimby shared some thoughts with me during our fun interview. She said, "If you lead with love, positivity will come back to you tenfold. It has a much greater impact. If you lead with anger and fear, you produce negativity. Reveling in the hurt only makes everything worse."

Given her life experiences, I'd say that's some really solid advice.

So, let's start living in love. Let's reshape our musings and relearn how to respect each other. Despite feeling frustrated when life doesn't go according to our strict plan, we can adjust, knowing it's okay to make mistakes and to be authentic, if not for acceptance and love then at least for our own sanity. When we stop adhering to impossible standards and start living life authentically, we can be free of the worst perfectionism has to offer: judgment, disdain, loathing, and disproportionate negative beliefs. Once we realize we are enough as we are, we can begin the journey to self-acceptance, self-love, and love and acceptance of others.

That's worth it, literally and figuratively, isn't it?

M

M IS FOR MISTAKES

How many of us are afraid of making mistakes?

I assume everyone reading this is probably raising their hands in unison here.

How many of us are hell-bent on not making them for fear of being judged?

Maybe fewer people now, but I'm still willing to bet it's the majority.

How many of us have convinced ourselves mistakes make us a bad person unworthy of someone else's time, attention, love, or validation?

Oof. That one hurts. I know I used to feel this way, and some of you may not even realize you do too.

When we strive to be perfect, we don't want to be wrong or cause anything to go awry. But what are we so afraid of? Why do we feel conditioned to never slip up?

Our friendly licensed psychologist from "The Anxious Achiever" podcast, Dr. Thomas Greenspon, explores the research grounded in this idea: "Perfectionists are afraid of being judged. Making a mistake means there's something wrong with you, so there's a defect involved... that means you're less acceptable as a person. Perfectionism is really a self-esteem issue... The meaning you give to making a mistake... means that there's something wrong with you... therefore, you will not be acceptable as a person. It goes very deep" (Aarons-Mele 2022).

But part of being human means making mistakes, so how are we supposed to live?

When I talked to Flame Schoeder about mistakes and why so many of us seem hardwired to freak out if we make them, she informed me this phenomenon could be routed all the way back to the beginning of human history. The fight-or-flight response in humans is tied to the fear of making mistakes. Quite literally, a mistake could mean the difference between life and death.

Think about it—you could face death if you chose the wrong hunting ground, selected the wrong plant to eat, or journeyed too far north instead of south. I don't know about you, but this revelation stunned me. It makes total sense, of course, but until she mentioned it I never would have put two and two together quite so powerfully as she did here.

Humans are essentially hardwired to run in the opposite direction of death, and thousands of years ago, mistakes could mean the end of your life or jeopardize the livelihood and safety of you and others. The fear we taste and the judgment we anticipate when we make mistakes in the short term is something that was ingrained in our DNA millions of years ago (Mark 2019). For our prehistoric ancestors, ridicule and exclusion served as punishment for making a mistake and, in the most severe cases, even death. Over time, those instincts apparently stuck with us, ingrained like etchings on a rock, locked in place, permanent and unwavering, even through millennia. Instead of fearing death from animal attacks or floods or a raging war, we are more frequently dealing with the fear of judgment, mockery, and feelings of being an outsider, unloved and unwanted.

Back to modern society.

If mistakes are necessary to achieve success, and perfectionists are attracted to success, then wouldn't it stand to reason that X + Y = Z? In other words, if perfectionists like success, and the way to success is to make mistakes, wouldn't we be making more of them? Why is it so difficult to embrace the unknown? Why is it so hard to be wrong?

When I was little, I said something that, to this day, my parents still occasionally bring up. I recall I was writing, and I offhandedly said, "If it were a perfect world, pencils wouldn't need erasers because we wouldn't make mistakes."

Seriously. Coming from a child's mouth. Those words probably should have sent me to therapy right away.

Instead, I recall my parents saying something to the effect of, "Wow, what a profound thought," or probably more like, "Huh, that's deep. You should write that down so you can remember one day."

Looking back, this was a signal and outward sign of perfectionism. According to Dr. Greenspon, I was afraid of making mistakes because of my fear of being judged and less acceptable as a person. He was correct in a way, and it did go pretty deep, and if I'm being honest, it still sticks with me today. After all, I remembered exactly what I said all those years ago, not on paper, but through muscle memory. It's like I can still feel the anxiety, the palpitations, the fear, the judgment. What I truly craved more than anything was acceptance, so I feared a mistake would mean people would be dismissive of me, ignore me, deem me irrelevant, less than human. Imperfect.

Much of my aversion to making mistakes was also due to social anxiety. Research has shown that perfectionists "with social anxiety pay more attention to details in interpersonal interactions, worry about making mistakes, doubt their ability to communicate, and often blame themselves for small mistakes, [so much so that] it developed into social withdrawal" (Fang and Liu 2022). Those who know me well today would never assume that as a young girl, I was terrified of picking up the phone to call a friend, or raising my hand in class, or just physically being in any social setting. I scrutinized cues and behaviors. I constantly worried about what others would think of me. I doubted my ability to communicate confidently. This would later translate into withdrawal from activities and pure avoidance of the things I believed I wasn't good at.

That sucks, right? To actively avoid or procrastinate from doing things just because of my own distorted sense of reality. Did I have proof I would suck at something? Nope. But did I have a strong conviction that I wouldn't be perfect? You bet. Did I avoid it? Yup. Is that a crappy way to approach life? Absolutely.

If mistakes are essential, but perfectionists hate making them, how can we shift that fear mindset to one of growth and acceptance?

Life coach Keri Martinez understands mistakes all too well and used to panic when she made one. She told me while she still has her *freak-out* moments, she at least recognizes that "the freak-out isn't ideal, and I start asking myself questions to get my brain to put the brakes on and take time to examine this." Stopping our brains from running rampant by asking questions is one healthy way to channel control and get a handle on the situation.

This is otherwise known as emotional agility. These "skills are an antidote to this paralysis... Stating your fears out loud helps diffuse them... Next comes accepting reality... Then comes acting your values" (Boyes 2020). We must arrest our unrealistic thoughts and stop them from spreading like a disease to the rest of our mind. Mistakes are part of the success equation, and without them, we wouldn't be learning and growing.

Mistakes aren't all bad. Keep repeating that to yourself over and over again. They are okay and a normal part of life. Mistakes can even make us seem less strict and uptight, and who knows, it might even make others like us more. But in all seriousness, as Alexander Pope famously said, "To err is human," so it's time to live up to our birthright.

Go on. I dare you.

N

N IS FOR NATURE

What does nature have to do with perfectionism? Not the essence of something or a disposition, but the actual, external environment?

Let's find out.

Perfectionists are inherently programmed to execute and accomplish as quickly and as flawlessly as possible. Fang and Liu describe them as those who "work compulsively and persistently toward their goals and measure their value solely on the basis of their output and achievements" (Fang and Liu 2022). Running a million miles a minute, always trying to overdo it, constantly blazing ahead, and for what? Are we really enjoying the ride? Are we really getting *more* done? Do we really feel better when we're going fast?

In the last few years, many sources have shown an increasing amount of research that advocates for outdoor time.

Why, you ask?

Well, for one, so many of us sit too much at work these days. Hours spent toiling at a desk or at a computer screen are where workers find themselves spending most of their work week. It has been linked to increased blood pressure, high blood sugar, excess body fat, unhealthy cholesterol levels... [and even] death from cardiovascular disease and cancer" (Laskowski 2022).

So, how does nature play into this exactly?

Plainly, it helps with "improved attention, lower stress, better mood, reduced risk of psychiatric disorders, and even upticks in empathy and cooperation" (Weir 2020). Not only green spaces (think trees, forests, grass, pastures, etc.) but also blue ones too. "The color blue has been found by an overwhelming amount of people to be associated with feelings of calm and peace. Staring at the ocean actually changes our brain waves' frequency and puts us into a mild meditative state." This is why people who live by water are more physically and emotionally healthy compared to those who don't.

Note to self: Move to the ocean.

One study I found particularly intriguing concluded that nature connectedness (NC) is indeed positively associated with eudaimonic well-being (EWB), and in one aspect in particular—personal growth. I should mention that eudaimonic means striving to achieve something difficult. Either way, "these results signal the important role NC may play in contributing to positive psychological functioning" (Pritchard et al. 2020).

Well, hell to the yes! Nature can be our solution to finally feeling good and functioning more beneficially.

The concept makes complete sense when you think about it—bubbling brooks, soothing winds from the trees, the chirping of birds, the smells of fresh air, the heat of sunlight directly on your face, warming your cold insides. Peaceful. Easy. Natural. Calming. There's a certain melody to it that gives us pause.

When life gets unmanageable, out of control, and downright depressing, I find it helps to take a walk in a quiet reflective place. Not down the street where you can hear traffic and voices and other distracting noises, but in nature—maybe down a path, or in a recluse, or sanctuary, or park, or a wildlife refuge. Notice how most of these words are inherently soothing? Recluse, sanctuary, refuge—all these nouns are describing places of peace or safety.

Sounds nice, doesn't it?

Growing up, I lived across the street from a cemetery. Yes, I know how creepy that sounds, but I actually found it to be very calming. Hardly anyone was there, but the solitude was extremely invigorating and refreshing. I heard only sounds of nature and silence. What a way to disconnect and slow down for a change.

Back in high school, I would often go for runs there—feeling the breeze hit my skin and billow through my hair, tapping into my body's energy propelling me further ahead, my arms pumping in synergy with my legs, the sound of my even breaths once I found my rhythm. I liked challenging myself and seeing what my body could do.

I used to go to escape but for the right reasons. Not to avoid, not to ignore, but to embrace, to appreciate, to slow down; to revel in the solitude and calm and remember I'm just a blip on humanity's radar.

In college, I ran among the trails and woods in rural New Hampshire, although this time it was to escape and avoid. I tried to forget how out of control my life was at a time when I was the most vulnerable and at my lowest weight. But even back then, the simple act of being in nature provided me with some much-needed time to think—to really ruminate on why I was torturing myself by starving and trying to become someone who just wasn't me.

Nature can help remind us of what's really important and bring us back to the basics. Out here, no one cares what car you drive, or what your job is, or if you have a million followers on Instagram. The trees and animals don't give a crap what your name is or why you're here, just that you are a part of the universe. There are no politics, to-do lists, or expectations. Just the simple act of being in nature, cohabiting in a place where we've been for millions of years. We don't compete, or think too hard, or get lost in stupid memes or arguments or meaningless tasks. We're getting lost in ourselves instead.

What a concept!

In a world moving light years ahead every second of every day, when phones are never turned off, when people are always on the go and have no break or moments of quiet reflection, it's refreshing to know nature is there to calm us, saying it's okay to take rest and relax and slow the hell down. I don't know how else or eloquently to put it, but being in nature is just that—natural. We should do it more often.

Now go get outside!

O

O IS FOR OVERACHIEVER

Interestingly enough, many people loathe overachievers.

They're usually over-the-top, intent on doing beyond what is expected, seemingly perfect, often judgmental, don't know how to set healthy boundaries, and expect the utmost from themselves and everyone else, leaving zero room for error.

Quite frankly, they can be a lot to handle. Pushing others aside, not out of anger or jealousy, but perhaps because they're so wrapped up in what they're doing that they forget to focus on anything else, or maybe they're focused too intently on the wrong things.

Let me explain.

For those overachievers who crave power, money, and recognition, a high-earning job is part of that equation, right? Personal and executive coach for high performers Keren Eldad did a survey of over 1,000 high-earners having a salary of at least $200,000 a year to evaluate their happiness and self-acceptance rates. What she found was over 53 percent of them didn't have everything they wanted, were jealous or even resentful of others' successes, and were deeply unhappy (Eldad 2019).

Quite the paradox.

More Americans are finding themselves less satisfied (a.k.a. happy) as time goes on. According to recent Gallup polls, this trend is continuing downward, with seemingly no end in sight. We are now at an all-time low of just 38 percent of Americans who are satisfied with their lives (Enten 2022). In another article by Eldad, the main source of dissatisfaction was this: "The constant pursuit of the illusory things we think we want produces strain to keep up, low self-worth, and general unhappiness" (Eldad 2019).

So why do we consistently want to outperform? Would that prove us to be better humans than everyone else? What would that really mean?

My personal belief is that if we're overachieving, we are likely compensating for something else.

In other words, we're ignoring something or someone.

Think about it—the very word *overachieve* signals that we're underachieving in other areas. Maybe we're scared of getting bad grades, so we hone in on socializing just a bit too much. Perhaps we're afraid of being rejected by our peers and colleagues, so we withdraw and focus on solo activities like going to the gym, watching TV, or traveling constantly. We may be too ashamed to admit we may fail at one sport, so we go all in on the one we know we can always win at.

In my early school days, I was the kid who would go home, do their homework, watch some TV, have dinner, and read a book before bed. Pretty boring by all accounts, but that was me. I craved a schedule and relished a routine. Looking back, I'm fairly certain I was afraid of making new friends and being social. There wasn't a playbook for that, and I was terrified of saying the wrong thing or doing something dumb where they might judge me or see me as someone unworthy of being their friend.

Even in sports, I was trying to outdo myself. From my Pop Warner (youth sports) cheerleading days until my very last competition in high school, I was all in on that sport. Technically speaking, my stunts, cheers, motions, form, and dance capabilities were top notch. My gymnastics and tumbling, however, could use some work. Even back then, I was willing to admit that. But despite still not feeling perfect at it, I could sense that leadership seemed to be calling my name, and dare I say I was captain material.

The night of my junior year banquet came when my coach would announce next year's cheer captains. I was about 90 percent sure my name would be called, so I prepped myself, got all excited, and was ready to smile and be proud after eleven years of hard work and overachievement.

Can you guess what happened?

Yup, she did not call my name.

I sat frozen in place, my muscles tense and unmoving for the rest of the evening, sitting there, shocked, stunned, disappointed, even mad. I couldn't believe my team couldn't see the years of hard work, sweat, tears, broken tailbones, sore muscles, black eyes, and sprained wrists I had put into the sport resulted in anything less than earning the title of captain. It wasn't even that I had worked hard, I had tenure! I was one of two in the group who had been a cheerleader the longest. For one of the first times in my life up until that point, I got my first taste of public rejection in front of my fellow cheerleaders, my coach, our parents, the football players, their parents, and their coaches.

Sixteen-year-old me couldn't bear the shame. I felt embarrassed, like it was my fault, like I did something to purposely jeopardize it. What had I done wrong? Did hard work not get rewarded? What was I missing?

It's interesting because I was also a jazz dancer, and a damn good one. I gave up dancing full-time after school to be a cheerleader in high school. I was faced with a choice of either/or, and I chose cheerleading. I wanted to be involved at school rather than at a dance company where I wasn't around my peers. And boy, at that moment, I deeply regretted that decision.

In college, I consumed myself with clubs, leadership activities, working out, internships, and, of course, rigorous academics to make sure I had as little downtime as possible. Why? To avoid and compensate. If I was constantly busy, then I wouldn't have to partake in the college rituals of making new friends, trying different things, and even partying. I attended a large public university where I should have been having the time of my life, but all I could think about was, *Am I involved enough?* Will that help me ignore the fact that it's tough for me to acclimate to this new environment? Can the overachiever in me work overtime to ignore the fact I don't really have a strong sense of self, of direction, of purpose?

Looking back, I know I wasn't alone. A 2022 student lifestyle survey found that over half (53 percent) of college students at the time of the survey felt either alone or isolated (Gingerella 2022).

Obviously, this would have been helpful information to have when I was going through that experience, but here we are.

So much of my life has been in pursuit of overachieving. And for what? What exactly was I trying to prove? That I was the smartest student? The best cheerleader? The perpetual leader? The workaholic? The thinnest college girl?

I wish I had asked myself those questions when I tried so hard to overdo it. But seeing the bigger picture is tough, especially when you're in the thick of things and can't always have a clear head.

For Paulette Piñero, this desire to go above and beyond in an unhealthy way was mostly due to survival. As a young girl, she found herself trying to take care of her mother and everyone else in her family. That pressure eventually morphed into overachievement by always trying to please and attend to their needs. In her youth and later into her teens, she didn't have the liberty of messing up because others depended on her. It wasn't until college that she finally shed that burden and spent time working on herself. It took her years, but she eventually founded her own coaching business in 2020 to help other Latinx business owners (mostly women) realize their inner strengths and use them to push through struggles to success.

Okay, so what is the antidote to overachievement?

It requires being vulnerable, being open to new experiences, and learning new things. It means being willing to do the work and take a hard look at ourselves and why we're ignoring something else or someone else. Better said, "Many high performers would rather do the wrong thing well than do the right thing poorly. And when they do find themselves in over their head, they're often unwilling to admit it, even to themselves, and refuse to ask for the help they need" (DeLong 2014).

It turns out we need to be the opposite of what we're used to, maybe even programmed to be. I'm not saying being vulnerable and open will come easy, but it's necessary to make progress if we want to see real change.

If we want to dial it back, we have to tune in—to ourselves, our feelings, our emotions. Dig deep into those dark corners of the mind. We must be willing to let our guard down and accept this small risk for something bigger, hopefully better.

For me, I wish I hadn't been so uptight or unwilling to bend to anything outside of my own personal distorted views.

If I hadn't focused so intently on perfecting my schoolwork, would I have made more strong, lasting friendships?

If I hadn't been so mad about not making cheer captain, would I have seen that I was still a good cheerleader?

If I hadn't immersed myself in so many commitments during college just to be busy or put on my résumé, would I have chosen some other path or passion?

Achievements and accolades can be outward signs of success. But what if I turned that energy and focused inward? Would I have realized I was compromising my own true happiness?

I'll never know what could have been, but you might.

As Eldad reminds us, "Aiming for achievements instead of a deeper understanding of yourself and what you want can cause you to miss the mark completely and feel utterly defeated in the end" (Eldad 2019).

Truer words were never spoken.

So go ahead—challenge your assumptions, redefine what success looks like, start small instead of reaching impossibly high, and celebrate progress no matter how tiny. Try mapping out what true, authentic happiness would look like for you. Think deeper. Look at the costs of fear that stop you from being innovative and creative. Stop being the superstar, and start being you—imperfect, flawed, empathetic, human. Get that self-esteem back.

No one has it all figured out, and none of us are perfect, so why aim for the stars when we can simply touch the sky?

P

P IS FOR PROCRASTINATION AND PARALYSIS

Procrastination and paralysis seem like the very antithesis of perfectionism.

So, then, why do we suffer from them?

On one episode of *The Anxious Achiever* podcast, guest speaker Eleanor Beaton recalls that it shut her off from taking risks and doing things simply for fun. As an author, leadership expert, and founder of a media company, it delayed actual progress. "I would have great ideas that I would sit on for a year or more. Not because I didn't have the capacity to do it but because I was being an anxious achiever, I was being a perfectionist, and I didn't want to play full out, in case I messed up, or something bad happened, and I couldn't control the outcomes" (Aarons-Mele 2022). She blamed it on not having the capacity to get it done, but in reality her desire for perfection ultimately deterred her from getting started (procrastination) and resulted in her not taking any action at all (paralysis).

But let's break these down a little further.

First, let's hone in on procrastination.

In a 2013 study, procrastination is defined as "the primacy of short-term mood repair... over the longer-term pursuit of intended actions" (Lieberman 2019). In basic terms, it's about short-term gain for long-term pain. And, of course, "perfectionism has been linked to various negative outcomes including... failure, guilt, indecisiveness, procrastination, shame, and low self-esteem" (Flett et al. 1995, 456). So, one could reasonably conclude that because they are so focused on impossibly high standards of success, they never reach them (because they're impossible), and therefore procrastinate getting them done.

But why? If we're aiming to be so perfect, wouldn't that translate to completing things on time and meeting deadlines, or perhaps even early? If we always like to keep moving ahead, why are we going backward or remaining stagnant?

Allow me to introduce you to our second player in this chapter, paralysis.

Ever heard of analysis paralysis? I'd be willing to bet many of you suffer from this.

According to Reclaim.ai, it "is the lack of ability to decide out of fear of making the wrong choice." This definitely resonates with me. It can feel like the worst-case scenario in a lot of ways. In another Reclaim.ai study that focused on task management specifically, they found that an overwhelming "78.7 percent of people experience stress due to increasing tasks and lack of time to get it all done every week" (Reclaim.ai 2022).

It's pretty wild when you think about it, because in 2023, we should be getting more done with the amount of talent, technology, and people we have available, and unfortunately that's just not the case. The task management study also found that COVID-19 negatively impacted our ability to stay focused. "Since the 69.7 percent increase in meetings that resulted from the pandemic, [individual contributors] are now only able to spend twenty-one hours a week on their actual productive work, which means almost half of their workweeks are being misallocated toward time not spent producing" (Reclaim. ai 2022).

TL;DR: There's too much noise out there to focus. And for perfectionists, this is even more difficult with our ongoing quest for flawlessness.

Boston Marathon bombing survivor and professional ballroom dancer Adrianne Haslet-Davis shares in a TEDx Talk why she procrastinates. As a self-proclaimed recovering perfectionist herself, she recalls early on in school she had trouble completing assignments on time, even though her work ethic was strong and she wished to achieve and get good grades. "It wasn't until my adult life that I learned procrastination is a trait of the perfectionist. The perfectionist is afraid of completing a task because it won't be perfect. I read that one day and it floored me... that is so true" (TEDxTalks 2015).

In 2013, years after becoming a successful ballroom dancer, she and her husband were enjoying a day off, watching the Boston Marathon runners, when suddenly the bombs went off. When she eventually saw her left leg gone and a sea of blood take its place, she realized something life-changing. "I thought that was it. I'm no longer Ginger Rogers. That's it. The dream is gone. And what's scarier than a dream being gone is not realizing that your dream actually came true and not celebrating it when it was" (TEDxTalks 2015).

Oof. That one hits home.

Raise your hand if you realized after the fact that something you did was actually good enough. Adrianne realized her dream did in fact come true, and instead of reveling in that feeling of accomplishment and joy while it was actually happening, she chose to ignore it, not celebrate it, and keep trying for more.

Of the many procrastination/analysis paralysis instances in my life, I think the one story that's most relevant here is this very book you're reading. As I'm writing this chapter, I never actually believed it would come to life. So many would-be-authors don't end up publishing due to a myriad of factors, but mostly because it's downright difficult to imagine completing such a momentous task alone. It's daunting to think of writing 40,000 plus words, marketing your book, selling it, getting a publisher and marketing agency and fans to buy into it. All that, plus the time and money spent on this one solo activity. It's beyond exhausting! So, we delay, we procrastinate, and unfortunately, many of us will never end up getting it done. But for perfectionists, the primary reason is we're too scared the end result will not be flawless. We're also afraid of being judged, or ridiculed, or found to be an impostor. So, like Adrianne, we fail to complete the assignment.

This very compilation I've created has been a work in progress for the better part of a decade, almost fifteen years. Through that time, I've written some, revised a little, created more, and then never touched a thing for years until this past year. It wasn't until that day at a conference in San Francisco that I felt like now was the time, like I was suddenly compelled to finish this once and for all.

Paulette Piñero and I talked about this other factor in paralysis—this juxtaposition, if you will—of paralysis versus urgency. As perfectionists, we are continuously firing on all cylinders because we feel we must win the race, so we go at top speed, but then again, it must be perfect, so we delay.

"This continuous tug of war...[happens]... We delay what we know is important because we can't make a decision because it won't be perfect, and then do too many things rapidly because we feel the need to do them fast and because we think others need it right away."

As she said this, I remember vigorously shaking my head, yes! Absolutely, I identify with you!

She thought, "If there's a mistake, there's only one chance to make it better. So perfectionism keeps you paralyzed." When she realized her expectations were unrealistic to the point where she could never enjoy any results, it dawned on her she needed boundaries. "If I can't see results, then it's very difficult to measure the impact. It cuts innovation and creativity. You can't see beyond what you believe is the ideal."

Okay—so what then? If we're in this cycle of decision paralysis (stopped), procrastination (slow), and then quick execution (rapid speed), how do we break free? How can we find ourselves somewhere more in the middle?

Paulette recommended, "Done is better than perfectly planned."

As I imagine Adrianne would probably say, completing the assignment is better than not doing it at all.

Paulette adds: "Focus on your intentions, amplify your voice, get clear on your purpose, and build connections with those who can help you achieve your goals."

Boom. I love it.

Simon Sinek, Brené Brown, and Adam Grant (three of my favorite experts on these topics) mention the concept of the *shitty first draft*, or SFD, on Simon's *A Bit of Optimism* podcast. Honestly, if you don't know these three, google them immediately. They are not only amazingly talented and knowledgeable experts, but you feel like they're your friends who understand you and challenge you to be better. The witty banter between them is quite remarkable.

The SFD is right in line with what recovering perfectionists should put into practice to prevent procrastination and paralysis. "Everybody knows the first pancake sucks, but you go through the motions to get to the third pancake, which is perfect. The idea, though, of celebrating the first pancake going poorly as a step toward just making pancakes, right, I think is a skill. Anne Lamott calls it the shitty first draft [SFD] ... we really celebrate the SFD, because without seeing [it], we don't see where the growth is" (Sinek 2022).

Cheers to the SFD!

We can't expect perfection all the time, especially the first time. What if we just allowed ourselves to simply start? Simply try? Simply put something down because something is better than nothing?

Like I'm doing now, I'm writing instead of not. Putting words on paper instead of keeping it all in my head, thinking it's not good enough or perfect enough. Because it doesn't have to be. I just have to take that first step and begin.

Make that first pancake, let it suck, and do it again.

Q

Q IS FOR QUESTION EVERYTHING

Perfectionists often think in very black-and-white terms.

Yes or no. Right or wrong. Blonde or brunette. Dunks or Starbucks.

There's no gray area, no in-between, no real room for us to ponder, get curious, and create new ideas. We don't typically ask what is or what could be, which is crucial in living a life less perfect yet more fulfilled.

How many times have you heard the below statements or expressions?

Go for your dreams! (But also: Have realistic expectations!)

Live for today! (But also: Plan ahead!)

Love the skin you're in! (But also: Here are some makeup and beauty products to better yourself!)

Express yourself! (But also: Know when to hold your tongue!)

Patience is a virtue! (But also: There's no time like the present!)

Conflicting, right?

How do we know what's fact versus fiction? What's right, and what's wrong?

Here's the short answer: Technically, there can be multiple correct versions, but more importantly, truth is contextual, multifaceted, and best arrived at together.

Growing up, I always tried to be the *good girl*, the *perfect one*. I never strayed far from the predetermined path. I did what my parents told me: I completed my homework on time, followed the rules, respected my elders, didn't argue, and fell in line.

Always.

It wasn't until college that I learned to think more critically, analyze more deeply, and question everything I once knew. Not because I wanted to be a moody, difficult teen but because it was necessary to find out who I wanted to be and how I could become a better, more well-rounded global citizen.

As a communication major, one of my classes was on the social construction of reality. I recall my professor saying that truth is not only complicated but that there are multiple truths (McNamee 2010). For a perfectionist who likes control, order, and simple, clear answers, this sounded like a nightmare! What do you mean there can be multiple versions of the truth? What do you mean what I've been taught all my life isn't necessarily the only truth?

For those who may not know what social constructionism is, let me quickly define it. Simply put, it's a "perspective which believes that a great deal of human life exists as it does due to social and interpersonal influences" (Galbin 2014, 82). In other words, our perceptions and definitions of the world around us are largely constructed via our interactions with others. Think of it as crowdsourcing in a way. There is no one dominating truth or fact. There is only what we collectively decide it is or won't be.

Sounds a bit out there at first, I know, but stay with me.

Back to my professor. One of her research papers states: "Constructionist forms of inquiry shift our attention from validity to utility and from uncovering facts to constructing useful ways of going on together" (McNamee 2010, 18). Truth and facts and knowledge are, then, socially constructed. So, if reality needs to be questioned, it behooves us to ask things like: What story is being told or what's not being told? Why is it being told this way? Who is the source? How old or new is the information? How useful is this and why? Is there any vested interests at play? How should *we*, not just me, define reality?

The reason this still flashes in my mind today is that I remember thinking for the first time it was okay for me not to have all the answers! It was okay for me to keep asking questions and to even doubt what was presented to me at face value. I didn't have to accept everything given to me as gospel, as the one source of ultimate truth. Instead, I could dig deeper, look at something from multiple perspectives, wonder and question, get curious, and ultimately make a well-rounded and well-researched decision through the help of others.

For Dima Ghawi, she learned to question everything once she realized that what she wanted (happiness, freedom, enjoyment) contrasted with the expectations and rules previously set for her. Growing up in Jordan, she was programmed to believe certain tenets and behave a certain way. Life was very much like a vase for her. You couldn't break it, and you needed to work very hard to preserve the perfect façade, even if the foundation represented anything but. Any small crevice or slight crack would be a tragedy, irreparable. It wasn't until depression hit her that she understood the need to change.

"Deep depression, that's when I started questioning my life and started questioning what I had been told, and how I am being judged, and every time I think about my life, it just confirmed to me that that was not what I wanted. So the first step was to question, to question everything." It took a mental health emergency to put herself first, to start creating a new narrative and reshaping her life.

Keri Martinez also talks about the importance and value of questioning what we know and what we are taught. Among other things, her strong religious upbringing greatly influenced how she viewed the world.

"There was always this idea that I needed to be perfect like Christ."

From education to career to parenting, she felt the pressure to be flawless in order "to have any kind of worth or value in this world... but you know, that doesn't work." After suffering a breakdown when her job became impossible to manage, she decided to seek outside help.

For Keri, this was especially difficult, because in her mind, "only crazy people see therapists or counselors..." In other words, she thought there wasn't anything glaringly obvious that convinced her she needed external support. Outwardly, she seemed to have it all put together neatly, cleanly, and perfectly. Inwardly, things could not have been more different.

Once she realized perfectionism was holding her back and that therapy could be for anyone struggling, she understood it was okay to question what your brain was saying. "Then, I started to realize: What else am I doing wrong? What else did I misjudge?" Once permission was granted, Keri allowed herself to start chipping away at those old messages ingrained in her for so long. She understood what didn't work for her anymore, what needed to change, and used this new frame of reference to create a new identity. There were other ways to accomplish and grow, not just one designated lane.

Unfortunately, many don't seek help when they encounter mental illness. According to the National Network of Depression Centers, $210.5 billion is lost in earnings each year due to serious mental illness (National Network of Depression Centers 2018). It's also one of the top three reasons for workplace issues alongside stress and family crisis. Luckily, both Dima and Keri used depression as the vehicle to move forward and make positive changes. It was the primary reason they both decided to break the mold and identify a new path. What they were used to, what they were told—it didn't have to be true if it didn't serve them well, or it didn't have to be the only truth.

If we committed ourselves to think in ways that were more beneficial, more open, and more diverse, then perhaps we could learn to relax and enjoy life more. Perfectionists are guilty of being so hard on ourselves that we sometimes can't see what else is out there. If truth is a social construct and there can be many versions of what's right, then we should be rejoicing instead of wallowing or stressing. We don't need to have all the answers, and in fact, we shouldn't! We should be like the cat where curiosity reigns supreme, except without the ultimate demise.

Ask, analyze, question, wonder—after all, aren't humans the only mammals with these unique capabilities? If so, let's use them!

R
R IS FOR RELATIONSHIPS

Not all relationships are created equal.

With our constant need to feel revered by everyone, perfectionists are often people pleasers and, I would argue, shape-shifters. We morph into different versions of ourselves depending on the person, the situation, the mood, etc. We hold our heads high and talk authoritatively when Person A is around, and act shyer or reserved when Person B is present. We tailor ourselves and our personalities according to what we assume the other person expects and wants, all in an effort to feel accepted, appreciated, and valid.

When I was young, I would modify my behavior, my voice, and my stance depending on my audience.

For my family and close friends, I was probably the closest to the real version of me—outgoing, personable, dependable, energetic, smart, trustworthy, loyal. A dancer, a bookworm, a writer, a cheerleader, a foodie, a runner, a spaz.

To most, I appeared very comfortable in my own skin. But, as a kid, it can be scary to put 100 percent of your true self out there. I remember acting way more confident than I felt to certain people who I wanted to be friends with, hoping they couldn't tell I was lying, scared to be the real me.

Around boys, I was a bit more timid and shy, not quite sure what I should do or say. I wanted to look cool, and I had zero clue on how to do that. I was also nervous that if I talked about certain things I knew nothing about (sports in detail, for example), then I would be found out and ridiculed, and that would suck, especially if I wanted to impress someone. It really does sound nuts on paper than in your own head, doesn't it?

Around authority figures like teachers, I was always the good girl who was polite and raised her hand in class, who turned in work on time or early, and who just wanted their approval and support.

Suffice it to say I was like Jekyll and Hyde, magically turning into one of my many alter egos, all so I could feel loved and valued, like I truly belonged.

Slightly altering your word choice or your actions to suit a particular audience or situation isn't necessarily bad.

However, when you please others and try to meld with their needs, you can become lost, a personality set adrift, floating from person to person, relationship to relationship, guessing what others need and adhering to that.

Author and psychotherapist Pete Walker calls this phenomenon *fawning*, or "the use of people-pleasing to diffuse conflict, feel more secure in relationships, and earn the approval of others" (Finch 2019). Often, it stems from unresolved childhood traumas that never went away:

Trying to compromise and overcompensate, feeling guilty and responsible when it's not really your fault, not knowing how to say no, or pulling back on relationships, even the one with yourself.

But hey, that's easier than risking a disagreement, tension, mental, or even physical, stress, right?

In a 2016 study on brain activity, Dr. Juan Dominguez of Monash University in Australia examined the effects of people pleasers' actions on their behaviors and relationships. He concluded that people pleasers, who are more likely to agree with others and compromise their beliefs and needs to keep the peace, hate to disagree with others. When they did, it resulted in immense mental distress and discomfort, which could lead to "poor decision-making, anxiety, or difficulties in interpersonal relationships" (Borreli 2016).

It looks like being a people pleaser is bad for relationships. Pretty certain we saw that one coming.

But now what? How do we get out of this mindset? How do we take ownership of our convictions and stay true to what we believe and what's important to us? How do we even know what that is?

Before we dig too deep here, let's touch on loving relationships for a moment.

Many songs are written about the topic. Some still can't figure the whole thing out, and others are so engrossed in it that they forget anything else exists. Love is a fickle, funny thing. No singular person is an expert. We all can have different opinions on it. What I think most everyone can agree on is that love is complicated and takes effort. Beyond that, it fluctuates, so it's okay that humans react differently to love. Even as a universal experience, it is one of the hardest terms to define.

In 2005, a groundbreaking Harvard Medical School study on love and relationships showed that "when we are falling in love, chemicals associated with the reward circuit flood our brain, producing a variety of physical and emotional responses—racing hearts, sweaty palms, flushed cheeks, feelings of passion and anxiety. In addition to the positive feelings romance brings, love also deactivates the neural pathway responsible for negative emotions, such as fear and social judgment" (Edwards 2015). Quite literally, love can make us blind—ignoring perhaps red flags we would otherwise see.

Now let's take this a step further.

Perfectionists often believe being perfect means being happy. It's as if we're in a relationship with it and falling head over heels in love, causing us to be unhappy, never feel like we're enough, always trying to achieve more, attempting to live up to impossible standards, holding us back from getting what we really want and deserve.

What if (as we should in an unhealthy relationship) we decided to break up with perfectionism?

When I spoke with our Latina boss Paulette Piñero, she brought up this very idea of severing ties. As a young child, she found herself largely responsible for providing for others in her family, and with an abusive father and a single mother, she was doing the best she could. She felt like she didn't have the liberty to be who she wanted because of expectations and obligations that she believed were solely her duty. Becoming a young mother herself at the age of twenty, by default she had to go all in. She focused on surviving and caregiving for her newborn son, who, it turned out, would have a severe disability.

As some years passed, she still desired to start a business and become a Latina entrepreneur. It wouldn't be until 2018, when she initially began writing a business plan to have on the back burner just in case it eventually turned into something real.

That day would come in 2020 after she almost died of COVID-19.

Lying in a hospital bed, hooked up to machines, forced to say a premature goodbye to her husband and kids, she thought, *God, if I live and survive this, there are so many more things I want to do with my life.*

It was at this moment she finally realized the need to put herself first. The relationship she had to focus on, the one she ignored for so long, was the one she had with herself.

"I realized that I needed to break up with perfectionism... break up with the things holding me back."

After a month-long stay, she returned home from the hospital and eventually started her slow recovery, inching closer to starting her business. Later that year, she launched Unstoppable Latina, a powerhouse leadership coaching program for Latinx CEOs who are making an impact and reimagining what success can look like. A business and strategy expert, she's been featured on Meta, Telemundo, and other well-known channels for the amazing work she's doing.

Let her success be a valuable lesson to us all. To secure your own happiness, you need to be conscious of what you feel and what you know or strongly think will make you happy. In a world where technology confuses us, bombards us with more information than we care to know, and introduces us to more opinions than we want to see, it's important for us to stay grounded and true to ourselves.

You can't make everyone happy in life, no matter what. Heck, Mother Teresa tried, but despite the fact the woman's a literal saint, she didn't have universal acceptance. Every relationship we have, including the one with ourselves, should be a place where we can feel deserving of happiness, regardless of outside opinions. We shouldn't feel the need to appease everyone all the time. It is impossible and tiring and, quite honestly, a waste of your time. And by the way, if you have relationships that don't fit into your life, take a page out of Paulette's book—do away with it! Break up with them! Fuhgeddaboudit!

S

S IS FOR SOCIAL MEDIA

Facebook. Instagram. Twitter. Snapchat. WhatsApp. Tik-Tok. LinkedIn.

These social media platforms are just some of the tools that bring us connections, meaning, purpose, and joy—all at scale. And yet, it can also lead us to feel even more alone or take us down some dark paths of insecurity, self-doubt, sadness, misinformation, or other horrible and troubling thoughts.

According to Simon Sherry, a clinical psychologist at Dalhousie University, it is especially concerning today, as "those social media images end up serving as yardsticks people can compare themselves to, and a perfectionist is always trying to keep up with the Joneses" (Aschwanden 2019). In a world where we crave acceptance, aspire to be the best in every way possible, value integrity and truth, and strive for the impossible, is social media a friend or foe? Can it be both?

It was late fall 2004 when I created my first social media profile on Facebook. It was the dawn of a new medium, one where information was shared, updated, consumed, and posted for posterity. Anything you chose to share was fair game for discussion, to celebrate, and also to mock. We unknowingly opened ourselves up to a wider audience, from acquaintances to family to complete strangers.

I remember joining when it was only for higher education institutions, and when my alma mater was granted access to the platform, I was stoked, hesitant, curious, but mainly excited to find out what all the fuss was about.

Fast forward years later and it's served two purposes, at least for me. It has provided access to people and information, and yet it has also been the source of unkind gossip, negative rumors, fights and tension, and just plain mean stuff.

I recall one instance where social media intervened in a very nasty way. After socializing outside of work a few times, I realized there was a completely different side to one of my colleagues, which was troubling and didn't seem to equate with the version she presented to the public. One night, I posted a status update on social media that had nothing to do with her at all, but she took it personally as an attack and went on the offensive. She sent me mean text messages, tried to spread false rumors, and even went so far as to invite all our other female colleagues out to eat and intentionally left me out. While I certainly didn't wallow that I wasn't included or that she misconstrued information and used it against me, it was, of course, hurtful.

Social media can be tough. Put more bluntly, social media can be a bitch.

There have been countless reports on the negative side effects of social media platform usage. In 2018, the Pew Research Center found that "59 percent of US teens have been bullied or harassed online, and a similar share says it's a major problem for people their age" (Anderson 2018). Additionally, 42 percent experienced some form of offensive name-calling, 32 percent have had false rumors spread about them, and 25 percent have received unsolicited explicit images, among other data points. As a vulnerable population, teens are especially susceptible to taking criticisms to heart. And, of course, yours truly got caught in these crosshairs!

Not only can social media bring out the worst in people, but it can spread disinformation. In a 2022 survey where nineteen advanced countries were asked about social media's impact on their populations, a whopping 84 percent believed social media and the internet made it easier to manipulate and encourage others to subscribe to false information and rumors (Wike et al. 2022).

So far, social media isn't looking too good.

For perfectionists, it can fuel the already raging fire of anxiety within us with more feelings of doubt, unworthiness, fear, worry, and depression. It can be tough when we see others achieving our dreams when we're struggling, especially when it looks so easy and effortless.

Mirror, mirror on the social media wall, who's the fairest (and prettiest, and richest, and best) of them all?

We feel inadequate and less than others and keep swirling these thoughts around in our crowded brain. We can also become frustrated when we see people validating fake news or their own twisted hypotheses, which can be dangerous. We become despondent when we're attacked or made fun of. It's just plain unkind.

Clearly, social media isn't all it's cracked up to be.

What, then, could possibly come out of it that's decent? After all this negativity, can there be a good side?

The short answer is yes.

According to Siddiqui and Singh, it "has increased the quality and rate of collaboration for students. Business uses social media to enhance an organization's performance in various ways such as to accomplish business objectives, increasing annual sales of the organization" (Siddiqui and Singh 2016, 74).

Other studies have found positive effects for youth and society at large. In a 2022 Pew Research survey about teen social media usage, 80 percent "say what they see on social media makes them feel more connected to what's going on in their friends' lives, while 71 percent say it makes them feel like they have a place where they can show their creative side. And 67 percent say these platforms make them feel as if they have people who can support them through tough times" (Anderson et al. 2022).

It has also been shown to increase feelings of acceptance, specifically within minority groups, as CNN reports that "Black and Hispanic teens were more likely than their white counterparts to report feeling more accepted because of social media" (Holcombe 2022).

Youth can stay connected and find support they may not have otherwise.

In general, society has benefitted from having a network that goes beyond geographical borders. Physical barriers are no longer an impediment to community, progress, and change.

During my conversation with Lindsey Pollak about social media, she had an interesting take. At the height of the pandemic, she decided to give up Facebook and Instagram because it was too overwhelming, and she didn't want to keep comparing her life to others. As a speaker and author accustomed to being on the road and engaged in events, suddenly she found herself constantly home and had fewer things to distract her attention. So, she felt bombarded by updates and didn't trust herself to be able to ignore all the negativity and comparing that perfectionists can be so easily prone to.

And yes, you can actually quit social media if you want to! Her general view is that there are two types of social media users: active versus passive. Active users use it for research (her example was using Pinterest to browse through dining room tables for inspiration) and have agency over it, creating a healthier relationship. On the other hand, passive users scroll through posts with no real direction or purpose and can spin out of control or go down rabbit holes, sometimes leading to depression.

In early 2023, she posted on LinkedIn (the only social media platform she has now) about buying new clothes to fit her new body. She mentions gaining a little weight and having to recalculate and pivot to a new wardrobe.

Instead of feeling shame and guilt, she chose to embrace it. There was an overwhelmingly positive response to her post, including comments from yours truly. Being vulnerable on social media isn't easy, but there is a whole community of supporters out there ready to affirm your worth and value. You do matter, you are wonderful, and the size of your clothes shouldn't dictate your importance as a human.

To answer our original question, social media can be both a blessing and a curse.

It can give us ways to connect beyond borders, create change, be creative, find long-lost friends and family, get information, and feel accepted and worthy.

And yet, it can lead to harmful behavior and outcomes.

Take the stories of CJ Dawley, Ian Mitchell, and Selena Rodriguez, who all died by suicide (Murphy Kelly 2022). Each of their families has filed lawsuits against Snap and Meta, the parent companies of Snapchat, Facebook, and Instagram, because they strongly believe their children's deaths all stemmed from their platforms. There's also been, in the era of Donald Trump, the dawn of *fake news* and individuals pushing personal and oftentimes biased agendas that can infect others with their distorted and dangerous beliefs.

When Lindsey quit Facebook and Instagram, she told me it was one of the best decisions she ever made. She feels lighter, happier, and really hasn't missed anything important. She still remains connected to the people in her life who matter, without the distracting yet addictive noise.

Perfectionists are prone to seeking attention and validation for our own self-worth needs, and it behooves us to know how to use social media knowledgeably and in a way that protects us from the trolls and the misinformed. Or you can be like Lindsey and quit altogether.

Either way, we must tread carefully in this virtual world of smoke and mirrors because there's always another side to the social media story.

T

T IS FOR TIME

A riddle: What stalls, yet flies? What seems to stop but also speeds up? What drags but then accelerates?

Answer: Time.

No matter how much time we get in a day, there's always something left to be accomplished. We can become anxious, reminded of how much we want to do but haven't yet fulfilled.

To put it bluntly, time is a slippery thief, robbing us and taunting us at the same time. For perfectionists, this is especially challenging because if we can't have enough, we'll never reach our goals, but if we have too much, we become frustrated by our own inability to speed it up or get things done faster.

Was it always this way?

According to Vanessa Ogle, assistant professor of history at the University of Pennsylvania, it wasn't until the arrival of the Industrial Revolution, with "new technologies like the railroad and telegraph, which made the world increasingly connected. Without accurate, globalized time, though, a burgeoning era of commerce and travel could have faced some serious roadblocks" (Sollinger 2016).

Before then, there wasn't much use in having a universal time structure. Other than farmers and sailors who needed to measure their days and nights by something more than the sunrise and sunset, nobody else had to know if it was 2:00 p.m. or 2:15 p.m. As society became more advanced and more dependent on one another for economic livelihood, people slowly realized the value of getting on the same page. Otherwise, we risked messing up schedules, shipments, trades, and more. Hence, universal timetables were born.

So, did aligning our time really make us better as a society?

Depends on who you ask.

In the United States, we treat it like a noun, like something we could hold in the palms of our hands. A previous boss once told me, "Time is your most valuable asset," and he's not wrong. But that statement also assumes we can control it, manipulate it somehow to our advantage, and even bend it to our will. Going back to our Protestant beginnings as a country, we were founded upon the principles of hard work, productivity, and individualism. That still very much holds true today, since "the average American employee puts in 260 more hours a year than the average British worker and 499 more hours than most French citizens" (John 2019).

As Americans, we spend most of our time tied down to our jobs, and for what? We're obsessed with being busy because we don't want to run the risk of being labeled lazy, which to a perfectionist is one of our nightmares, right?

As long as we focus on being the best possible version of ourselves at every waking moment, we'll never have enough time to complete our tasks, be the best we want to be, achieve everything on our goals list, and more. There's too little time and so much to do! On the flip side, we're taunted by time's slow crawl itself.

So, how can we shift our mindset in a healthier way? Can we shake the yoke that time holds over us?

When I studied abroad in college in the south of Spain, I wanted to give myself a very authentic experience. Like a true perfectionist, I had to go all in.

I decided to stay with a host family instead of living with other American students in a residencia or dorm-like hall. I pushed myself outside my comfort zone and traveled to new places with friends I only met at the start of the semester. I spoke the language in class, with my peers, with anyone, even if I fumbled through it. I tried new foods, and I even dreamt in Spanish!

Side note: Turns out I actually like morcilla, or blood sausage. Don't worry, there's no actual blood in it.

Most importantly, I learned that time meant something different there. It didn't have to be maximized, stretched, or measured. It could just be.

The Spanish are proud of their culture, one that makes rest and relaxation a priority. No one seemed to be caught up with measuring every ounce of time. Everyone seemed more relaxed, casual, devil-may-care. Deadlines were more of a suggestion, meeting up with people at a certain time was more of a target, and like the Guadalquivir River, nobody was in a hurry. Sure, there were the occasional business folk who were tied to the clock a bit more than the average Spaniard, but in general life moved at a more manageable pace.

What I realized is that above anything else, they valued balance—time spent working was fine and honorable, but family, friends, mealtimes, rest times, and the simple act of enjoying life in all its beauty were more important.

I hardly ever napped as a child. My mom still recalls when her friends who had babies the same age as me would relish naptime. All my mom could say was, "What the hell are you all talking about? My kid never sleeps!"

In Spain, I didn't have much choice with the *siesta*, a widely recognized and enforced nap time for everyone. Most shops, restaurants, and businesses would be closed in the midafternoon hours. I said I was going all in on study abroad, so I decided to give the *siesta* a try. I was incredibly shocked to find not only did I sleep, but I was more rested, recharged, and ready to tackle the remainder of the day.

I would have thought I lost time and wasted it by napping, but it turns out that with more sleep, I had more patience, I lived in the present moment, and I was even able to solve my own problems without completely losing my shit.

On the flip side to this, when I spoke to my friend and fellow published author Roger Osorio, we talked about how perfectionism shows up in relation to time, and he had some interesting and eye-opening theories.

He posited, "What role does time play in perfectionism? If we're so focused on trying to be the best and perfect at one particular thing, then how can we channel the same positive energy into another project that is required of us without completely breaking down?"

Mind blown.

He's right, of course. If we're spending all our time on one project to do it perfectly, then inherently something gets left behind or suffers a less-than-perfect fate.

We may also risk burnout. In professional settings, perfectionists can seem like an employer's dream: willing to go the extra mile, wanting to produce exceptional work, meticulous, likely to stay late, etc. At first, "employers may get top-notch results, but in time, this can also result in burnout for them and even those around them who are burdened by their unrealistically high standards and seemingly unreasonable expectations" (Main 2023). Despite putting in more time, perfectionists are often the first to fall.

We simply cannot do it all.

As much as we've tried, as much as we want it to, time doesn't just bend to our will. Despite our best efforts, it will keep at its regular pace, chugging along like a train, just coasting. We can't fight against it, and we can't help it along. We have to be good with what is happening in the now.

Instead of being worried about what we cannot change, focus that energy in the present.

Ask yourself: Is that deadline your own, or someone else's? If it's someone else's, are there other things getting in your way preventing you from finishing that task?

Can the project be good enough without having to be perfect?

Can you give yourself some grace and be patient with the journey?

Do you need help to get it done?

Can you recognize that not all good things can be done quickly?

If you think the answer to any or all of those questions can be yes, then you're on the right track (train pun intended).

Time needn't be our enemy. It can, in fact, be something in the background, floating in existence, not serving as a source of worry or anxiety, just there. Not taunting or chastising, but cheering us on.

U

U IS FOR UNDERESTIMATE

One would assume perfectionists are naturally super confident and self-assured all the time, but that can't be further from the truth.

While the outside world might think we have it all together, we tend to underestimate our own abilities, skills, values, and, in general, ourselves.

If we constantly strive to be the best and reach for the stars, then why do we greatly undersell what we're truly capable of? What are we afraid that might signify?

As you might expect, this happens more frequently to women than men. As evidenced in *The Atlantic* article, "The Confidence Gap," there is a plethora of research and studies demonstrating the shortage of women's confidence levels when it comes to industry selection, promotions, raises, and more. For example, Linda Babcock of Carnegie Mellon University found in her study of business school students that "men initiate salary negotiations four times as often as women do, and that when women do negotiate, they ask for 30 percent less money than men do" (Kay and Shipman 2015).

In that same article, a 2003 study on the relationship between female confidence and competence found that when offered to participate in a science competition, "the women were much more likely to turn down the opportunity: only 49 percent of them signed up for the competition, compared with 71 percent of the men because they are less confident in general in their abilities, that led them not to want to pursue future opportunities" (Kay and Shipman 2015).

A final study proved that men applied for a promotion if they only met about 60 percent of the job description, whereas women believed they needed to meet every criterion. In this context, "underqualified and underprepared men don't think twice about leaning in. Overqualified and overprepared, too many women still hold back. Women feel confident only when they are perfect. Or practically perfect" (Kay and Shipman 2015).

And that's a problem.

If women are consistently doubting their ability to succeed or even get the chance to succeed, then they're inherently missing out on important milestones and opportunities. This, of course, can translate into lost income. As the Pew Research Center has shown time and time again, "the gender gap in pay has remained relatively stable in the United States over the past fifteen years or so. In 2020, women earned 84 percent of what men earned" (Aragão 2023).

That's nuts, right? Even after all the progress we seemingly have made in recent years, we are still living in a world where it takes women, on average, about forty extra days of work to earn what men do in a year.

In a world that is inching toward making positive strides with diversity, it seems we're continuing to fall short.

In my interview with Dima Ghawi, she taps into this idea of women, in particular, underestimating themselves a lot. Part of her story, if you remember, is that she grew up in a culture that prized men over women, resulting in her believing women were less than, that they had to fall in line and do what was expected of them without rocking the boat. They had little to offer outside of home skills and providing for others. When she realized she greatly compromised her identity because of these expectations, she turned them around and flipped the narrative. What if she could become confident in herself, assured she was worthy and just as capable as a man?

Unstoppable Latina CEO and boss woman Paulette Piñero also admits it takes some work not to underestimate yourself. As a business owner who grew up having to provide for her family at a young age, she understood the challenges that came with great responsibility. And yet, despite successfully getting through tough times, she still believed she wasn't enough. The seeds of doubt were sown deep, and it took her a while (and a life altering event) to change her mindset. Only when she looked death in the face during her battle with COVID-19 did she realize that doubting herself was not an option. She needed to have confidence in the life she had built, the family she had, the unique talents she possessed. She was worthy and decided to finally act like it.

Looking back on my time studying abroad, I realize it was the first time in my life I felt completely uninhibited. No one to boss me around, no one to tell me what was right or wrong, and no chance to be afraid and wallow in my fear and anxieties.

Maybe it was the fact I knew my time was limited there. Maybe it was because everyone I knew was 3,000 miles away, or maybe I was just fed up with my own impossible standards. Maybe it was a combination of all three. Call it cultivating my vacation self—learning to be as I wanted, not what was right, expected, or assumed. As I opened up to new experiences, I found myself shedding layers of doubt and insecurity, like I suddenly found my mojo and stopped underestimating myself.

I decided to book a weekend trip to London with two other girls from my study abroad program. During the planning, I let go of my control issues and decided to let them pick the hotel. At first, I was a bit uncomfortable because the place they chose had no reviews and no pictures. Definitely not somewhere "old me" would have selected. But, staying true to the new version of myself, I went along for the ride.

When we arrived in the early morning hours and pulled up to the front door, I could tell something was off. The place looked fine, the neighborhood appeared safe, but when we walked in, nobody was at the front desk, and after about thirty minutes of searching, we couldn't locate any hotel worker in the building. There was a basement with some lights on and a dude watching TV, but he wasn't affiliated with the hotel, and honestly, he creeped all of us out. It was official. We were stranded.

Rather than freak out or cry or call my mom back home, I embraced it. I realized it wouldn't do me any good to lose it now, and I needed to solve the problem immediately in front of me. I tapped into the knowledge I didn't know I had. I took the reins and ushered our group outside to start brainstorming a solution.

Upon looking around, I saw a Holiday Inn billboard not too far away. As one of the other girls started to cry, I told her we should start walking in that direction and not to worry. We'll be safe soon. As we navigated toward the sign, we passed by a small boutique hotel that looked open. I told the other girls to wait, walked in, and explained the situation to the manager on duty, and he had a room for us available. Thank goodness!

But what I realized was despite feeling incapable and not overly confident, I actually did have it in me to be strong, brave, and savvy. Getting locked out of our hotel in a foreign country at two in the morning taught me resiliency, street smarts, and that I was powerful, a leader, and nothing bad actually happened.

To this day, I still think about that time in London with admiration. I took what was a very stressful and potentially unsafe moment and took control of it using the knowledge and skills I inherently didn't even know I had.

As Glennon Doyle would say, we can do hard things!

So what's the moral here?

If low confidence breeds inaction, and inaction can lead to lost opportunities, then we must find a way to embrace the confidence that already exists within ourselves, especially women.

I contend agency is the antithesis of underestimation. We need to own it—like actually try to take a risk, make a choice, decide on a project, or commit to a schedule, whatever it may be, to move forward. As we've seen, action is better than inaction because at least we land somewhere. And if things don't work according to plan, that's not necessarily a bad thing. We can use those failings as learnings, mistakes as teachable moments, and late realizations as motivation for next time.

Of course, perfectionists struggle with agency largely in part because we're convinced nothing is better than something imperfect, or we risk being wrong, two scenarios that make us wildly uncomfortable. However, "the irony is that striving to be perfect actually keeps us from getting much of anything done" (Kay and Shipman 2015). If we're both the problem and the solution, rectifying underestimation starts with being cognizant of the issues at hand, understanding that we are powerful and capable, and taking action.

As Nike so famously says, "Just do it."

And you know what? I'm starting to realize it's true.

V

V IS FOR VULNERABILITY

Allowing others to see who we really are is tough. For perfectionists, it's like having people view us under a microscope—peering into our souls, judging, assessing, assuming.

If connection is why we're all here, if that's what makes us human, then why are we so afraid to show an ounce of imperfection? What do we have to lose?

Perhaps one of the most famous researchers and storytellers of our time, Brené Brown, has some rather profound thoughts on this topic. Rather than view vulnerability as a negative, she views it as something that gives us power, that opens us up to feeling worthy and accepted. Which is a bit contradictory, right? I mean, if vulnerability means we're opening ourselves up, aren't we exposing something? Leaving gaps? Admitting fault?

Brown doesn't think so.

In her TEDx Talk on this subject, she encourages us to "lean into the discomfort," and that "we can't practice compassion with other people if we can't treat ourselves kindly." Makes sense. "We pretend that what we're doing doesn't have an effect on people, but it does" (Brown 2010).

We can pretend to have it all together, but we don't.

We can pretend we're perfect, but we're not.

We can pretend everything's okay, but it's all right when it isn't.

We can pretend vulnerability isn't scary, but for many of us, it is.

What are we so afraid of?

In a world that runs on high speed with the weight of a thousand expectations and suggestions, it's tough to break through the noise. It's hard to admit we don't have it all figured out, or that we're scared or don't know all the answers. We desire certainty and struggle when we can't find it. We want to feel loved, accepted, and safe.

If humans need connections, and if we're living in a uber-connected world thanks to the internet and social media, why aren't we more comfortable sharing and opening up?

My junior year in college, I remember someone from one of my classes coming up to me and saying, "Hey! You're, like, super fun. I had no idea. You seem so serious all the time in class that I never expected to see you out at parties. But you're actually fun!"

The first thing I thought was, *Uh, thanks, I guess?* But I also felt sort of offended. I knew I could come off as a bookworm, a little too intensely focused on my academic experience, but I didn't know my classmates and peers assumed I was a recluse. Damn!

I wanted to shift that perception because, contrary to what this person thought, I didn't have it all figured out, or put together, or know everything. Sure, I was intelligent, but that didn't mean I couldn't have another part of me that liked socializing, dancing, and enjoying life. You could actually do both. When my classmate shared that, it made me realize it was okay to let others in and allow them to see the more vulnerable, more open, more genuine side of me.

Permitting others access to view this more tender version was a bit scary at first. And yet, that comment made me realize I unintentionally alienated people. That needed to change because I didn't want to be that person who made everyone feel like they had to walk on eggshells. I didn't want others to be intimidated, undervalued, or stand-offish because I would never want that for myself either.

Deep down, we all have insecurities and questions and doubts. So why hide them?

When Lindsey Pollak and I discussed this topic of vulnerability, she mentioned something that stuck with me. She said, "Vulnerability is actually a tool in my anxiety tool kit. Because when I use it, I always feel better."

Wait, what?

When she wrote her first book and submitted her manuscript to her editor, she recalls him saying to her, "Did you ever do anything wrong? Every single thing you described doing, you did perfectly. You're not gonna help other people by being perfect. You're going to help them by telling them when you messed up and fixed it and how they can do it too."

So, showing our vulnerability actually makes people want to learn from us? That seems antithetical, right?

But it's true. People don't want you to be perfect. They want you to open up and share things that might be difficult or personal but also real. Embracing the good, the bad, and the ugly, and everything in between, lets others in, shows them you're human (i.e., not perfect), and provides them with the confidence and autonomy to share their own struggles and stories.

Lindsey sums it up like this: "The more vulnerable and imperfect I have become and admitted to being, the more successful I've been. Without fail."

In the corporate world, sometimes this idea gets lost on us. We think that by sharing more and exposing our innermost thoughts, someone might take advantage of that and use it against us. I've certainly felt that before. If I asked a dumb question, shared my struggles, or admitted I didn't know something, that might lead to me being teased, penalized, judged, or deemed unworthy of the role.

And I'm not alone.

A 2022 Gallup survey found that just 32 percent of employees were engaged, reaching a new low that hasn't been seen since 2015. On the flip side, 17 percent of employees cited themselves as being actively disengaged, a rate not seen since 2014 (Harter 2023).

Despite these bleak statistics, vulnerability in the workplace has proved to be more effective and can even result in furthering one's career, as Lindsey well knows. A *CNBC* article notes, "not punishing mistakes, but instead analyzing and learning from them... has been shown to benefit a company's productivity" (Blumberg 2018). To use a specific example, "when Shell implemented [a] training company-wide over a fifteen-year period, its accident rate declined by an astounding 84 percent." Training made the workers feel more connected with each other and less hesitant to ask for help when needed. In turn, bosses benefitted by having stronger KPIs, more engaged and confident employees, and a more inclusive culture that prepared and nurtured rather than one that punished and promoted negativity and doubt.

As Brené Brown says, "There is no courage without vulnerability...[it] is not weakness. It's the ability to show up and be seen. It's the ability to be brave when you cannot control the outcome" (Balch 2021).

Amen.

Giving ourselves the permission and courage to be vulnerable is vital if we hope to shift the narrative from negative to positive. Vulnerability is a superpower, and if we become more accustomed to using it, the better or healthier we all become.

So shed your perfectionist armor and embrace the vulnerable in you!

W

W IS FOR WEIGHT

This chapter contains maybe my darkest secret.

For so long, I worried sharing it would make me look less intelligent than I really am, as if I should have known better. I worried others would judge me, make assumptions, look at me differently like I was permanently flawed.

For years, I denied anything was wrong, and even today not everyone close to me has any idea about the extent to which my desire to control my weight severely impacted my health and life. Although eating disorders aren't exactly topics that come up in casual conversation, I'm choosing this time to tell my story. After all, I promised to come clean and share helpful stories that could aid others in their perfectionism journey, and this is a big piece of mine.

From 2004 to 2018, I allowed my weight and those pesky numbers on the scale to be a torture device, a reason for me to feel intense shame and judgment. And yet, it was a time when I felt oddly empowered and in control. For fourteen years, I allowed myself to be a pawn in the game of power and sexuality, self-worth and love.

When we're little, the baby rolls, dimples, and general chunkiness are considered cute and endearing. As we grow up, suddenly the narrative shifts. We must eat the right amounts, not indulge too much, be active, and, above all, look trim.

Girls and women, in particular, are exposed to constant messaging about their appearances starting at a very young age, to the point where those messages become ingrained in our DNA. Mass media, of course, plays a big role in this. As Levine and Murnen state, "There is a wealth of evidence from content analyses that the ideal female body showcased on television, in movies, in magazines, and on the internet reflects, indeed embodies, the proposition that 'thin is normative and attractive'" (Levine and Murnen 2009, 15).

In the summer before high school, I started to become very self-aware of the shift in my weight and body. It was hormones and puberty, sure, but it was the first time I remembered feeling so uncomfortable in my own skin. I became self-conscious, mindful of the subtle but noticeable ways my physical appearance was changing.

Around this time, I realized I looked very different compared to other female characters on TV. My elongated and narrow face, crooked smile, shapely thighs, super large muscly calves, and the way my eyes weren't symmetrically aligned when I smiled—I couldn't find any of them represented in the media. What bothered me the most were my calves. I felt like everyone had smaller ones than me, even men, which was embarrassing.

I tried exercise. I stopped eating. I even attempted squeezing off the circulation with athletic bands. Nothing seemed to work, though, and I became extremely depressed.

Starting at a very young age, females are targeted with subliminal messaging that our bodies are not our own and need to be shaped, toned, trimmed, cut, and morphed into something for others' viewing pleasure. Case in point—Grand View Research found that global cosmetic surgery procedures is expected to grow "9.6 percent from 2022 to 2030 to reach USD 145.7 billion by 2030." In 2021, they noted for the US in particular, "Breast augmentation procedures increased by 48 percent, while the use of Botox injections increased by 845 percent" (Grand View Research Inc. 2023).

Fat is ugly, thin is pretty. Symmetry is beautiful, and asymmetry is unattractive. Anything that looks out of place on that canvas needs to be replaced, tweaked, or ripped apart.

According to the National Eating Disorders Association, "Perfectionism, having to follow the rules, and concern about mistakes [are found to be] much more common in women who developed eating disorders than women who didn't" (National Eating Disorders Association 2021). It makes sense, of course. Our quest to have the perfect body aligns with our desire to be in control and punishing ourselves when we make even the smallest of mistakes, taking even the tiniest bites of food, allowing the most minuscule of crumbs to enter our mouths.

In my conversation with Keri Martinez, her journey for the perfect body came out of a need to quell those suspicions that she wasn't enough. She was beating herself up for not reaching her impossible standards, and how did that pan out? Not well—the diet was not successful, and she felt worse off than before. Eventually, she realized dieting and trying to be a certain size were not working and not sustainable.

Since society doesn't enforce the proper etiquette when it comes to body image (read: acceptance), it's often difficult to gain ground and make improvements by eating to achieve a healthy figure instead of the skinniest one. According to the 2017 Dove Global Girls Beauty and Confidence Report, "54 percent of all girls globally do not have high body esteem... [For Generation Z specifically], girls with low body esteem and confidence [have] distorted ideas around their appearance [that] may lead to damaging, destructive, and often secretive behaviors around food" (Willer 2017).

It's sad to read that over half of girls around the world feel inadequate in some way. It's especially hard when we have so many different people telling and showing us how to look. I mean, come on! Why should I be listening to others' opinions about how I look and feel? Don't I have any type of ownership or say in what is best for my own body?

Growing up, eating was always a big part of my family's culture. My mom's side is large, loud, and Italian-proud, where it's essential to stuff your face or else it's a sin. I grew up hearing things like, "You have to finish your plate," and "There are starving kids in Africa," and, if I looked too skinny, it was "You're gonna wither away! Here, have another bite."

I never really learned to eat with ease, relaxation, or anything synonymous with enjoyment. I consumed in rapid motion: fast, scarfing every bite, and stuffed after every meal. I guess I was supposed to feel that eating was fun, a social activity, a time for family to come together at the table and share stories about their day. And it was, to a certain extent. And then college hit.

In the fall of 2004, I moved to another state, living with strangers, without a car to go home anytime I wanted, and was expected to just jump right in—academically, socially, emotionally, physically. I don't know what I expected college to be in terms of all that, but I definitely thought I would have an easier time adjusting. After a month or two of trying to fit in, I found it exhausting trying to keep up a lie. Classic perfectionist me attempted to morph into a different version of myself for multiple friend groups—the problem was, this wasn't my small town anymore. This was a large university with 10,000-plus students. My old people-pleaser playbook was suddenly rendered out-of-date.

I felt scared, anxious, and nervous, like I was losing something. It wouldn't be until years later when I realized that something was me.

Back to fall 2004. I couldn't keep up the façade any longer, and I began to feel overwhelmed, a bit panicky, and out of control, like my life was spiraling downward and yet simultaneously propelling forward without my permission.

To counteract how I felt, I decided to seek refuge in the one thing I thought I could control—my weight. I figured if I could physically become what I saw on TV, shed some extra pounds, make a drastic change, then someone (boys, friends, peers) would notice me, want to be around me, and everything would fall into place.

Sounds perfect, right?

Wrong.

Even perfectionists have prisons. In our minds, we equate perfection with power, security, and control. Being regimented about my eating was a way to maintain rigor and calm over a life of insecurity and instability, and one that felt like it was rapidly rocketing away. Lots of change, lots of new experiences, lots of things I didn't know how to deal with. Life became a game of waking up thinking about eating, going through the day counting calories, and maintaining the perfect number, all until the last moment of consciousness before sleep. Dreams were my only escape.

In the winter of 2004, during my first holiday break, I believed I was finally starting to look like what I had always desired, that perfect female actress on TV. Part of my brain told me I was on the right track but had more work to do, and yet another side told me this was not sustainable. I could tell I was unhealthy and couldn't keep doing this forever.

When I got home, my mom told me she bought me a new bathing suit for an upcoming vacation. I tried it on, excited to show her how much weight I had lost. I thought she'd be proud of me, given how hard I'd worked.

I'll never forget her response.

She broke down in tears.

She took one look at me in my bikini, skin and bones, my hips jutting out, my face gaunt and pale, the energy zapped from my eyes, and said, "Oh honey, what happened to you?"

To make matters worse, when I returned home that summer after completing freshman year, I had a scary moment at the doctor's office. During my annual physical, I remember feeling lightheaded and weak, which I was accustomed to after starving myself for months. The doctor took my blood pressure and stopped, looking confused. She tried again, and the same response. A third time, and she finally said, "Vanessa, I'm sorry, but I can't find a pulse."

If you think that would have terrified me enough to stop, you'd be wrong.

This eating disorder went on for fourteen years.

Yes, you read that correctly. Fourteen whole miserable years.

After that initial plunge into the eating disorder pool, I found myself wading in it for way too long, gasping for air, sputtering on fumes, kicking my legs to try to get above it all. I lost friends, caused fights, missed opportunities, and wasted so much time.

But I craved the attention—the looks, the stares, the whispers, the compliments, the jealousy. At least people were talking about me. I finally felt normal, like I belonged. Like I mattered.

Of course, those feelings of pride were fleeting. Always craving more, I was never truly satisfied.

Funny thing was, I've never felt lonelier and more disconnected and depressed than when I was anorexic. Almost like an out-of-body experience, I saw the despair in myself, like a heavy cloak weighing me down with the force of a thousand expectations.

At one point, I was so deeply sad and hopeless I began to understand why some people take their own life. What I felt was constant misery and isolating melancholy so much that I could rationalize the idea of suicide.

And that completely frightened me.

I did try to get help.

Therapy off and on for years, telling a few close friends and family what was really happening—I even attempted to stop using laxative pills for a little while. Like any true addiction, nothing seemed to stick.

It wasn't until I finally came to terms with the fact I wanted to have kids, my husband wanted to have kids, and my body needed to be healthy and nourished for life to grow. Suddenly, it wasn't about just me anymore. Once I realized that, I somehow started to let go of the old eating disorder mentality and move on with my life.

Was it an easy transition? No. Did I decide one moment to stop, and it just magically happened? Course not. It took the better part of a year to finally begin the weaning process. But the end goal was important, too important, I'd argue, and I wasn't going to risk my vanity and sacrifice my unborn children. They needed and deserved a healthy mom, and it all started with fixing this problem once and for all.

While I'm happy to say I'm fully recovered, I know those years wreaked enormous havoc on my mind, body, and soul and negatively affected those around me.

And I'm one of the lucky ones—not everyone's journey ends with recovery. Some find refuge too late, and some never get the chance to beat it.

Ultimately, you never know what people are thinking, who's judging you for what, or what your outward appearance means to somebody else. Whether it's jealousy or insecurity or happiness or indifference, it shouldn't matter. No study out there has found a direct correlation between a level of perfect weight and perfect life. The simple reason is that they don't exist. We keep fooling ourselves into trusting that these narratives ingrained in our minds for so long are the dominant and desired ones.

Your appearance has nothing to do with your future. It doesn't dictate what comes next. A healthy body does. It allows you the freedom to do what you need it to do—to live.

At my lowest weight, I was still convinced I wasn't thin enough to lose just a little more. You can never be too skinny, as they say.

But then what? Would that five-pound additional weight loss have resulted in me finally being happy?

Think we all know the answer here. Definitely not.

It's because, as perfectionists, we're constantly chasing the impossible, and when it comes to weight and eating disorders, there is no line we won't cross, no number low enough to get us to believe we are worthy. Weight and worth are so closely tied together here. And it's high time we sever that relationship because it isn't working.

I had fourteen years to mull over exactly why I developed an eating disorder. Over two decades later, I've realized I never set out to lose weight and get anorexically thin. Instead, it was a time in my life when I was thrust into a new setting, woefully underprepared for what to expect or how to react. My inability to adapt to my surroundings fueled my desire for stability, and I got it by focusing on controlling the one thing in my power—what I ate. I didn't choose to have an eating disorder. Nobody seeks it out. Rather, it's a byproduct of something else—usually a need to feel accepted, loved, worthy, good enough. All things perfectionists in their classic, most basic form crave.

At this stage in my life, I have accepted I am imperfect, constantly learning and growing, and resiliency, empathy, and humor are good qualities not to be understated.

I am proud to be standing in my own skin, the number on that scale and societal expectations be damned.

I've realized I only want those in my life who make me happy and are willing to call me on my bullshit. I now crave honesty and simplicity. Life doesn't have to be so serious or complicated.

So my parting words to you: Remember you are beautiful, you are worthy, you are magnetic. You are a human who deserves every bit of love and light as the rest of us. No one is that unique or special. We all leave the world the same way. If, after all that effort, the destination is set for everyone, then the journey should be way more fun.

X

X IS FOR EXPECTATIONS

I used to feel everything had to be in perfect order.

Clothes put away in drawers, papers tidied, cabinets shut, dishes washed, floors cleaned, laundry done, toys in bins. Growing up, it was expected of me. As I've grown older, I now realize cleanliness doesn't have to be equated with perfection. After all, what will be accomplished if the house is clean? What does that signify about me? Is my worth as a person tied to how clean my home is? Am I a bad person for leaving things messy?

Perfectionists put enormous pressure on themselves to accomplish tasks and collect accolades, like getting all A+'s, having the best job, or running a sub-four-minute mile, all things that sound great on paper but are pretty difficult for the average person to achieve. It almost feels as if we're setting ourselves up for failure automatically, and then we act shocked, even get angry and frustrated, when we don't meet them. Ever heard of the phrase, "You are your own worst enemy"? There's a reason for that—it's true.

I've learned to let certain things go over time. Especially after becoming a mom for the first time, I realized I couldn't be spending my time cleaning the kitchen floor and sweeping up every little crumb if I wanted to spend time with my son. Yet today, with two little boys, I still can't quite shake the desire to meet my extraordinarily high expectations. I mean, I have a goals Post-It note by my desk, for crying out loud, and what's on there? "Join a board. Publish a book. Present at a conference. Earn a spot on Boston's 40 Under 40." Totally reasonable goals.

Why do perfectionists expect the most out of themselves twenty-four seven? Why can't we ever just be content with what is happening now, or what we already have, or what might be more possible instead of impossible? And who are those expectations serving? Certainly not us!

So is it worth the stress?

I'd argue 95 percent of the time it's not. Because when we don't meet them, we begin feeling inadequate and guilty, like we should have known better. As a result, discouragement and hopelessness settle in and may cause us to give up altogether. And for what? What was I trying to achieve with being organized? Did it make me feel better about how out of control things seemed? Did it make me happier? Did I get an award? No, no, and still no.

So what do we do when we can't reach those lofty expectations? Do we freak out and spiral, or do we adjust, work around them, and lower them?

You guessed it—the latter.

But let's take it a step further: How do we lower our expectations in a way that doesn't make us feel like we're giving something up yet also allows us to still be true to ourselves?

Yikes, that's a tougher pill to swallow.

In Lindsey Pollak's book *Recalculating*, she addresses this concept of lowering expectations: "If you expect perfection, you will almost always be disappointed. But if you expect imperfection, you will be less discouraged when it happens—and thrilled when those expectations are exceeded! Lowering your expectations doesn't mean giving up on your dreams. It means giving up on the belief total perfection is possible. It means setting realistic goals" (Pollak 2021, 82).

It's that realistic goals piece that is so important.

But what are realistic goals, and how do we know the difference?

According to Indeed.com, "A realistic goal is one that you can reach given your current mindset, motivation level, timeframe, skills, and abilities. Realistic goals help you identify not only what you want but also what you can achieve" (Indeed Editorial Team 2022). For perfectionists, this means better understanding the lines that distinguish goals from being realistic to impossible, which, as the article states, really depends on a number of factors for each person.

For example, knowing I wanted to publish a book was a big goal of mine, yet I expected to be able to do that relatively easily and quickly. Was that realistic and reasonable?

Hell to the no.

I knew nothing about publishing, marketing, editing, or basically any step a traditional author would take. Combine that with the fact I was working full-time, raising two young boys, and managing our home. It all made writing this book a massive, daunting task! Per Indeed's guidelines, that goal would be dead in the water by now.

But, instead of ditching it and freaking out that I would never be able to get there, I decided to lower my expectations a bit and reassess what I could or could not reasonably do. I needed to reshape that big aspiration into smaller, more workable and attainable steps. If I had the mindset, motivation, and writing skills, then I could figure out how to make the time to turn this monster of a goal into a more comfortable one I could actually reach.

In my discussions with Paulette Piñero, our Unstoppable Latina, we explored this difference between attainable and unattainable goals. She mentioned, "If we're operating under everyone else's expectations, it cuts innovation and creativity."

In other words, if we're not allowing ourselves to formulate and share our own unique ideas because we're boxed into one mode of thinking, then new ideas never surface. If we prohibit creativity and innovation, then how would things change, and how would we grow and learn? Isn't that a sign of progress, even success?

An article in *Psychology Today* examines the idea of low expectations and the effect they have on reality. The article shares a study that highlights discrepancies between their subjects' expectations and their real experiences with video games. What they found was pretty intriguing.

"On average, those who liked the game less than expected gave 25 percent lower ratings overall compared to the zero-score group. But those who liked the game more than expected gave 43 percent higher ratings, on average, compared to the zero-score group. And those who initially saw negative reviews of the game and then said they liked it more than expected given, on average, ratings 62 percent higher than the zero-score group" (Jern 2023).

What do we make of all of this? Preconceived negative notions really affect how you view things. Said a different way, perceptions can strongly influence reality. If your mindset and expectations are negative, so will your reality be.

What about others' expectations of us? What then?

In the Curran and Hill study that examined over 20,000 college-age students, "Young people's perceptions of their parents' expectations and criticism have increased over the past thirty-two years and are linked to an increase in their perfectionism" (American Psychological Association 2022). Yikes! So if our parents exude high-expectation energy, and we now exude high-expectation energy, what will happen to future generations? It's like the heavy weight of it all gets passed down to the next generation but magnifies and worsens with each one.

So what does this all mean?

If you go into a situation on the lower end of the expectations spectrum, and the actual experience turns out to be better than you thought, chances are your sentiments about the whole thing are probably higher than they would be if the opposite occurred. In other words, if lower expectations mean our mental achievement bar is set lower, then we may be pleasantly surprised if things go better than initially planned. If the stakes are lower and the result is a winner, then we feel pretty darn good about ourselves!

Gambling is a perfect example of this. If you're playing roulette and the minimum bet is $5 at one table and $50 at another, wouldn't it be better if you lost everything at the $5 table? You put less in, so you didn't lose as much as you would have at the other higher-stakes table. I suppose it depends on how much you're okay with losing, but that's a different conversation altogether.

This mode of thinking also has the potential to lower our stress levels, therefore helping decrease anxiety and increase overall well-being. In a UK study that measured the correlation between happiness and reward, "the researchers found that day-to-day well-being does not reflect how well things are going, but whether things are going better than expected" (Moss 2020). Turns out that a good day is good if we believe it might have turned out differently (a.k.a. worse) and it didn't!

Sometimes, expectations need to be lowered for life to be more manageable and allow us to enjoy our day. Doesn't sound too difficult, but for perfectionists it can seem like a monumental task. But like goals, and unlike Texas, they're better when they're not bigger (Kidding—I love my Texas people). Lower the bar, lessen the stress, be pleasantly surprised.

There's also another alternative—having no expectations. That can sometimes be fun. Assume nothing, expect nothing, and watch and see what happens.

No matter how you spin it, we have choices when it comes to expectations. We can have high ones, low ones, or none at all. It's completely up to us. That is the agency that we can, in fact, control.

As you may have deduced at the beginning of this chapter, the word "expectations" doesn't actually begin with X. I had to deviate a little from my original plan of having each chapter begin with each letter of the alphabet. Just like having a clean and orderly house, I've had to readjust my expectations to live my life in a more fulfilled, meaningful way. In true embracing perfectionist form, I decided to let go of my rigid structure.

There aren't too many words that begin with X that I could have used here. But this title encapsulates the very essence of this book: If something doesn't fit exactly as planned, pivot. Get creative, and don't let it stop you from forging a purposeful and enjoyable path ahead.

Y
Y IS FOR YESTERDAY

Looking back, I would have done things differently. (How many times have we heard that before?)

As a kid, I used to focus so much energy rehashing and reexamining the past—seeking ways to live vicariously through my former self in the "good old days" or torturing myself by mulling over memories and mistakes, berating myself for not being perfect the first time around.

In 2022, a research study "found that adults make an average of 122 informed choices every day—but that doesn't mean the decision is final. A staggering 87 percent of those polled admitted to changing their mind" (Jurkschat 2022). And that's just informed choices!

Other studies now "suggest the average person makes an eye-popping 35,000 choices per day. Assuming most people spend around seven hours per day sleeping, that makes roughly 2,000 decisions per hour or one decision every two seconds" (Krockow 2018).

Sounds a bit ridiculous, but also overwhelming.

With so many decisions, it's no wonder some of them are about regret, what could have been instead of what really happened. Especially for perfectionists, we often look backward and wonder: Did I say the right thing? Did they judge me for that? What if I acted more confident, would they be my friend then? What if I make a mistake?

On Glennon Doyle's podcast, there's an episode where she, Abby Wambach (American soccer star, Olympic gold medalist, and Glennon's wife), and Amanda Doyle (Glennon's sister) discuss what it means to repair or say sorry. They talk through what it means to look back at yesterday and wonder if we can get a do-over when things go awry.

First, let's take the word "repair." Derived from Latin roots, *re* means *again* and *parare* signifies *to make ready*. For all you etymology geeks out there, this is pretty interesting stuff.

As Glennon, Abby, and Amanda mention, often when we look back and want to say sorry, we are asking for an impossible thing to happen. If repair means to make ready again, or essentially, to put back in order, then how can that be feasible when the past already happened, and there's nothing we can do today or tomorrow to change that (Doyle 2021)?

Profound stuff, right?

Time is a thief. We know this already. There is no way we can go back and reorder and reposition how or when things happen. So, if we're mulling over our thoughts and wondering if we need to apologize to repair relationships that may be strained or broken, we can't ignore that the facts are the facts, and despite our best intentions, we can't will the past to change on its own and reshape history.

For perfectionists, apologizing and admitting wrongdoing means we open ourselves up to being judged. Apologizing to someone means we made a mistake, we failed, and therefore we are a shitty person and imperfect and flawed. All terrible things in our minds.

If we can't look back and change what we wish we could, what should we do instead? Is there a path that allows us a chance to examine what happened but in an effective way?

Absolutely.

The Latin word *parare* means to make ready but also to prepare. The antithesis and opposite of repair is to prepare. If we can't repair and fix what was broken, then the next best thing is to prepare ourselves: to learn from the past, to embrace change, and to figure out what to do next.

If you can't alter yesterday, consider what you can apply in future scenarios to positively impact today or tomorrow.

I learned this the hard way with my eldest son's food allergies. After the initial shock wore off, I realized beating myself up and wishing I could go back in time to prevent them wouldn't change anything now. It wasn't a productive use of my time. I say this to my husband frequently: We can't keep blaming ourselves and rehashing what already took place. For better or for worse, food allergy life is our reality, so now we have to adjust and try to get on as best we can.

Remember my friend Monica from college?

It wasn't until after her skiing accident that she realized she had a choice. During recovery, she had the option to wallow in self-pity, rehashing the past, or to look ahead.

She chose to embrace the latter.

After taking a year to focus on her rehabilitation, she graduated from UNH not only with her bachelor's degree but later her master's degree. She went on to become first a biology professor, then made a big move from Maine to Florida and joined adaptive sports teams to continue her passion for athletics. She even earned a spot on Team USA, playing Paralympic ice hockey (she has medals!). It was through these activities and connections that she was able to secure sponsors to help finance renovation projects at her new home, which she purchased and owns by herself!

Quite simply, she transformed, creating a whole new life for herself, one she never realized was possible until the yesterday life she had suddenly wasn't anymore. She morphed from an able-bodied athlete to a Paralympic powerhouse!

When I told her about this book, she knew it was a lifelong goal for me and was excited to cheer me on. She's definitely someone I consider a true champion, a friend who not only shows up and roots for me but encourages the next step, listens intently, pushes me harder, and challenges me. She's turned into a woman I genuinely admire and respect. I informed her of my plans to include her in this chapter.

"It's not an option," I told her. "You're going to be in it, so just letting you know!"

She laughed. "I'm honored. But you know what? It took a really, really long time. It wasn't always this way. And I had to shift my mindset early on. I had to recognize that life would not be the same. But that also meant it didn't have to be negative and sad."

When I finally nailed her down for an official interview, she said a couple of things that stuck out.

"I couldn't look backward and focus on the past. That old life was gone, and I needed to relearn how to do the things I once loved in a different way. I was a woman in sport then, and I'm a woman in sport now. There's no difference that I see. The work and effort and determination are all the same."

Seems simple enough, yet beautifully deep and poetic.

So, if focusing on the past doesn't help, yet perfectionists are constantly trying to reexamine anything that goes wrong, how should we disrupt the cycle and harness our energy in a more positive way?

According to Martin Smith, a university researcher in the UK, "Perfectionism doesn't automatically resolve itself as someone gets older, and in fact may become worse as people age" (Aschwanden 2019). Because we continuously focus on the shortcomings of our repeated failures, perfectionists can adopt a bleak view of their past, which persists over a long period of thinking this way.

So, it would be wise for us to consider the opposite—not obsessing over the past so much. It sounds easy and trivial, I know, but rehashing what happened in the past only ever briefly works. Despite mulling things over again and again, berating ourselves for not achieving a different, more perfect outcome, things will not change by simply continuing to ruminate about it. Like Monica, we need to rise above, shifting positions until we find our footing again.

Maybe that means altering the way we define reality.

Maybe that means saying goodbye to old relationships or toxic friendships.

Maybe that means standing up for yourself when you previously couldn't find the strength.

Maybe that means letting go of old, tired expectations that no longer have a place in your life.

After all, there's only so much we can repair or make ready again. Instead of always fixing, let's focus on preparing for a better, more quality life.

Z

Z IS FOR ZOOM

My last riddle to you: What word can be used as two different parts of speech that connote different experiences?

Hint: It's in the chapter title.

Zoom, as a noun, of course, refers to the technology most of us are now accustomed to using almost daily for school and work thanks to COVID-19. As a verb, zoom, in this sense, refers to the speed of our own actions and thoughts, wanting to do more and achieve more as quickly as possible.

Let's start with the noun.

In my interview with Lindsey Pollak, she and I got to talking about the aftermath of COVID-19. Specifically, we spoke about the first six or so months after the disease was officially declared a pandemic and how many of us had to adapt to new technology to perform our jobs. Suddenly, there was this difference in classification of *essential workers* (those who had to be at their workplace and could not work from home) and *nonessential workers* (those who could either work virtually or those who were deemed redundant or furloughed).

For those of us who were nonessential workers trying to do our jobs the best we could, it was definitely not easy. Especially for full-time working parents like my husband and me, there were so many times where we felt 50 percent parent and 50 percent worker. We could not do either one of those tasks at 100 percent capacity. Every day, we had to split our attention and dedication to two important and taxing things, both of which required tons of energy, focus, and patience.

For nearly all Zoom users, we were obliged to slow down while also seeing our reflections on repeat.

For Lindsey, using Zoom drove her crazy at first. "It made me more conscious of my appearance because I'm constantly staring at my own face. It made me more anxious and insecure because I would focus on all the flaws."

In a purely virtual setting, you're able to see not only your audience but yourself as well. How many times have you focused on your own face and expressions in a meeting? How many times have you fixed your hair or worried about the shirt you had on, were concerned about how you positioned your head on the screen, or second-guessed what might be in your teeth after that poppy seed bagel? Yeah, probably should have chosen something else for breakfast.

I know that happened to me too many times—and let me be honest, it still does. I examine every detail I see in that little box on the screen and make sure I like what I see. Because my appearance equates to my worth, right?

A Stanford University research study found, "When you see a reflection of yourself, you are more critical of yourself" (Ramachandran 2021). So many of us are staring at ourselves rather than other people on these video meetings for hours a day. "It's taxing on us. It's stressful. And there's lots of research showing that there are negative emotional consequences to seeing yourself in a mirror."

So yeah, staring at our reflections can hurt. And in more ways than one.

According to Grand View Research, the pandemic has had a significant effect on the aesthetics medicine market (a.k.a. cosmetic surgery). "Remote working has increased the time spent on Zoom calls. People are paying attention to their physical appearance closely. This has increased the demand for cosmetic surgeries, with Botox being one of the most preferred procedures" (Grand View Research 2023). Seeing our faces reflected back to us over and over again augmented the appetite for cosmetic surgery to rectify our perceived flaws.

So not only did COVID-19 attack our bodies from the inside out, but it indirectly made us more uncomfortable and self-conscious, so much so that many sought refuge in elective surgery.

Seems very messed up.

As if that weren't bad enough, one 2021 study in the journal *NeuroRegulation* found that almost 94 percent of undergraduates had "moderate to considerable difficulty with online learning... At work, virtual interactions appear to cause two main problems (besides basic unpleasantness): lower performance and suppressed creativity" (Brooks 2022). That sucks on both accounts, especially since perfectionism has been on the rise, most severely amongst younger populations like college-age students.

Solution?

Take a break, pause the video for a moment, feel free to multitask and not look at yourself the whole time, fixate on things other than your own face.

Above all, recognize what you see virtually isn't necessarily the real thing and that screen time shouldn't replace face time. Plainly speaking, seeing one window doesn't mean we have the whole picture, and in-person interactions are almost always better and more satisfying than those on screen.

Time to talk about zoom, the verb.

Perfectionists can't seem to grasp the fact that when they do things quickly, we may not produce top results. I'm sure you've all heard the phrase, "Slow and steady wins the race."

Perfectionists tend to zoom through life, not paying attention to our surroundings or the fact that someone else might get ahead because of our inability to stay focused. In short, doing something fast isn't always the most efficient or effective way and can distract us from completing it altogether.

I can personally think of way too many times where I've zoomed, and it didn't turn out so well. Case in point: One day, I was driving home after dropping my sons off at daycare and was trying to go quickly. I prefer to only slow down or stop if it's really necessary. Yes, I know, that's not a good outlook to have, but hear me out. I'd rather slow down a little bit instead of stopping. What's the point of hitting the brake when you can still coast?

Anyway, I went a little too quickly around a turn in a relatively new development and hit the curb. I heard a noise and thought, *Oh crap, that didn't sound good.* Sure enough, as I drove on about one hundred yards down the road, I noticed my car was off-kilter, so I pulled over, parked, went around to the passenger side, and you guessed it— flat tire. And it wasn't like I could get away with driving on it since I was only about a half mile from home. The curb had apparently punctured through the rubber enough to create a big gash.

Lovely.

I was so intent on going fast that I ended up delaying my whole morning. And for what? Was zooming through my drive really necessary? Did it provide me with an opportunity to save time?

Obviously not.

Yet even podcast hosts can speed through an activity and feel as if their day is now ruined. In an episode on why perfectionists like to appear busy and do things quicker than they probably should, there's a moment when host Morra Aarons-Mele shares a very funny and super relatable story about a box of cookies. She tells us that one afternoon, she felt a bit out of control and tapped into an old bad habit. She ate one cookie, then two, then rapidly consumed the entire box. She was so passionately mad about it afterward that she felt intense shame. Her words were, "Well, now I've blown it" (Aarons-Mele 2022).

I nodded my head in solidarity when I heard that. I've done it more times than I care to admit.

It's almost as if our tendency to do things at breakneck speed is covering up our real feelings about ourselves. You might say perfectionism can disguise itself as avoidance. You might be saying, Huh? That doesn't make sense.

But let's dig deeper.

Rushing around, going too quick, being busy, and trying to accomplish and achieve as much as possible can masquerade as running away from something else, almost as if we're avoiding our true anxiety and fear.

Fear of what, exactly?

Well, I think that depends on each individual, but here are some questions we can ask ourselves to find out:

What am I seemingly avoiding?

What am I afraid of?

Why am I feeling shame?

How can I reframe the narrative around being busy means being perfect?

Remember the story I told in my introduction, the one where I kept loading and unloading my backpack on the first day of third grade?

This is a classic instance of perfectionism showing up as avoidance, fear, and shame all in one. By looking busy and doing things quickly, I delayed facing my peers because I was scared of embarrassing myself and being the center of ridicule and shame for not being on time to class. If I continued to look occupied, I could make myself appear smaller, insignificant, and blend into the coats and backpacks and shape-shift my way out of being there.

A bit more meta than that, though, I think it came down to this: I wanted to be accepted by my new cohort. I had the same teacher and classmates for first and second grade, so when third grade arrived, I wanted to impress and be accepted. I never got that opportunity that day, all because of that damn bus.

As we've seen throughout this book, perfectionism is not an easy thing to shake. It tends to stick with you for life, like a scar that won't heal or a permanent tattoo, although I hear nowadays you can get those removed.

The point here is this: If we're accustomed to doing things fast, then we must ask ourselves tough questions: Are we really getting done what we need to, or are we using this mouse wheel of movement to redirect our energy and attention away from something else that matters more? Are we hiding? If so, from what? And then, is it really that bad to just face it? What's the worst that could happen?

Take it from me: Don't speed on turns or through life. It doesn't tend to end well.

CONCLUSION–PARTING IS SUCH SWEET SORROW: A SUMMATION OF WISDOM

When I first started writing this book, there was still so much I had to learn.

I didn't believe I had the knowledge or even the authority to offer advice to others (impostor syndrome). I was afraid to fail and not write the perfect thing (failure/mistakes), so I delayed a little bit and started doing tasks I knew were easy to complete but didn't really get me any closer to my writing goal (procrastination/paralysis). The quintessential perfectionist trying to outdo herself (overachiever), I had high hopes and assumptions about what the book would turn out to be (eXpectations/goals). I wasted too much time scrolling online (social media) and even began to feel a bit angry and pissed off at myself (emotions) that I even considered doing this project when I already had a demanding full-time job and two young boys bursting with energy.

Had I gone too far?

But what I never considered was how this book would make me feel—not just accomplished or proud of fulfilling a lifelong dream, but finally free, living a life in truth rather than fear.

All my secrets, worries, anxieties—they don't hold me back anymore. I can confidently say I have nothing left to hide. It's all out in the open, and I'm embracing it.

But I know I'm a rarity.

As we've seen, perfectionism affects so many people globally and will continue to multiply and spread if we don't act quickly.

So, what are some key takeaways that we can deploy now? What have we learned?

- Too much ambition can be detrimental. Reality check it.

- You don't always have to be the best. Good can be good enough.

- We only control about 20 percent of our day, so we might as well embrace chance and the unknown.

- It's okay to take some time and discover who you are and who you want to be, even if it's not what you expected or were taught. You have ownership over your own narrative.

- When emotions aren't regulated well, it creates an imbalance that's tough to rectify. So take care of your feelings. Lean into them. Listen to them.

- Failure is not a negative thing. Learn to respect that failure is just one side of the same coin as success.

- Goals are good to have and even better when they're small and manageable.

- Hope can seem silly and vulnerable, maybe even risky. But perfectionists should welcome it.

- Impostor syndrome affects so many of us. We're all human with something to say and share, so let's start being confident in that. No one has all the answers.

- Contrary to what our culture believes, your job does not define your worth. Say it louder for those in the back!

- It's never too late to help teach kids today about resilience, about how to be okay with making mistakes and softening their expectations. They'll likely be better and stronger adults for it.

- Love and acceptance don't always go hand in hand. It's even harder to have both for yourself. But when we stop adhering to impossible standards and start living life authentically, we can be free of the worst that perfectionism is.

- Mistakes aren't always bad. In fact, making them shows we're learning and growing.

- Spending time in the great outdoors really does the soul and body good. You should try it more often.

- Being an overachiever usually means we're compensating for something else. Focus that energy inward instead of outward, and you'll see that accolades and accomplishments don't mean as much if we're not truly happy.

- Getting something done is better than not putting anything down at all.

- Life isn't as black and white as we think. It's all gray. So go ahead and question everything—analyze, wonder, ask, be curious.

- The relationship that is most important is the one you have with yourself. Once you feel comfortable in your own skin, you can take on more.

- Social media can be constructive and community-building when utilized the right way. No going down rabbit holes, and no comparing yourself to others! Perfection online is not reality.

- Time is a social construct. This doesn't mean we can create our own versions or speed it up or slow it down. All we can do is look ahead and keep going.

- Perfectionists underestimate their own confidence levels and capabilities most of the time, especially women. If we are to shift this narrative and mindset, we need to recognize that we know more than we're willing to admit.

- Vulnerability is actually a superpower, not a liability.

- Your weight does not equal your worth. Say that again, and again, and again.

- If you expect less, you're more likely to be pleasantly surprised.

- Rehashing the past only helps briefly. Looking backward is often dangerous and impedes progress.

- Zooming through life is no way to live. Steady as she goes, and don't always focus on your own face. There's more to the picture and to life.

This is really just the beginning. For you, for me, for all sufferers out there. To learn, to adapt, to grow, to move on.

Perfectionism has many definitions, but I see it as the intersection of two competing mindsets: striving for excellence (achievement) while also having a fear of failure and making a mistake (shame). These two forces are in constant battle with one another, forcing us to spend tons of energy trying to satisfy both when, in reality, it's an impossible task.

Now that we have some stories and advice from those just ahead of us to forge a new path, we can embrace who we are (natural perfectionists) instead of being ashamed. We can appreciate that our intentions are usually good. It's just our methods and mindsets that need a recalculation. A shift in energy and focus, we can get to a healthier place.

Look, my life still isn't perfect. It never will be. But that's not the point of this book.

I still deal with hard things.

I still experience pain and challenges.

I still sometimes fight with people I love despite not always knowing why.

I still don't always say the right thing.

I still get mad and annoyed at my kids.

I still worry, freak out, and fly off the handle every once in a while.

I still don't have all the answers.

But instead of pretending that I do, I'm starting to accept that I can screw up and get messy and not know the solution ahead of time. Now I know the world won't suddenly implode.

What I've learned throughout this process is that living in freedom, truth, and vulnerability is so much easier than living in captivity, fear, and control. And trust me— it's way more fun!

Well, I promised you a satirical A–Z guide, and what kind of perfectionist would I be if I didn't deliver?

ACKNOWLEDGMENTS

To my family and friends—you know who you are. I appreciate you more than you could ever imagine. Great books aren't written without lots of work and a little bit of sacrifice. Thank you for sticking by me and cheering me on!

To Eric Koester—thank you for pushing me to do this. I'm so grateful I had the courage to speak with you after that fateful conference in San Francisco. Thanks for your guidance and encouragement, and to everyone at Manuscripts LLC for having faith in me and my idea. I am indebted to your support and unwavering commitment to see my project through.

To Suzan Brinker—I am forever thankful to you for being a fantastic beta reader! I appreciate the time you took out of your already busy schedule to read through my first draft and make some suggestions and edits. A colleague and friend, I am honored you chose to be on this journey with me. I can't wait to read your first novel!

To my interviewees, Dima Ghawi, Keri Martinez, Roger Osorio, Paulette Piñero, Lindsey Pollak, Monica Quimby, and Flame Schoeder—you are all incredibly talented, inspiring, and kind individuals. I am blessed to have met all of you and will always be appreciative of your time, thoughts, and ideas. I learned some amazing things during our conversations, and this book would not be as rich and robust without you. I am always your champion, your cheerleader, your friend. Thank you!

Finally, I want to acknowledge everyone who supported me so graciously and generously in my presale efforts:

Emma Adelman
Marisa Alvarez
Stephen Amato
Darcy Anderson
Jill Baker
Jordan Becker
Lauren Bell
Shannon Belseth
Adam Boyle
Kelly Breitenwischer
Jason Breitenwischer
Suzan Brinker
Traci Brinling-Osowski
Jennifer Brouillard
Marissa Budds
Evan Buhler
Tammy Bush
Heather Campelia
Kara Capossela
Kendra Connolly
Tarrus Crew
Jessica Dang
Hannah Davis
Jamie Donovan
Melissa Falone

Marina Falone
Bethanne Falone
Steven Fanara
Pat Fligge
Andrea Gamel
Janna Gilpatrick
Jane Gould
Elizabeth Grella
Ali Harding
Shiro Hatori
Brianna Holt
Stefani Horton
Shannon Howard
Austin Hsu
Beverly Iuliano
Sharon Kahn
Stephanie Kattas
Lauren Kinnan
Kathryn Kissner
Eric Koester
Nicole Kulakowski
Elyse Kurzberg
Nguyet Labenski
Stephanie Lagace
Elizabeth Lamport

Victoria LaPlante
Sarah Lewis
Dan Loughrey
Marion Lovett
Jacobi Martin
Kaitlin Mattes
Marianne Maurer
Becca McGarry
Anna Meliones
Erica Moon
Casey Morlé
Matthew Nguyen
Katie Niro
Delia O'Donnell
Suzy Pallotta
Michelle Parker
Debra Parrella
David Parrella
Stephanie Pavao
Jen Pearlstein
Jared Pierce
Laura Pinkham
Lindsey Pollak
Kristen Pouliot
Monica Quimby

Nadia Quimby
Jose Ramirez
John Ricci
Meghan Ryan
Joshua Schock
Shivam Sharma
Courtney Shaughnessy
Karen Shields
Katy Smith
Renea Smith
Amy Spaisman
Carissa Spigner
Sarah Theriault
Dawn Tocci
Susan Ursch
Brianna Wahl
Kristen White
Jeffrey White
Pamela Williams
Scott Williams
Marcia Williams
Matthew Williams
Vivien Wu
Patricia Ziino-Fanara
Lisa Ziino-Mobilia

This book would not have been possible without your overwhelming support. It truly takes a village, and I'm so touched I can call every single one of you part of mine. Thank you truly from the bottom of my heart!

APPENDIX

INTRODUCTION

Curran, Thomas and Andrew F. Hill. 2017. "Perfectionism Is Increasing over Time: A Meta-Analysis of Birth Cohort Differences from 1989 to 2016." *Psychological Bulletin* 145, no. 4 (Dec): 410–429. https://doi.org/10.1037/bul0000138.

Mental Health America. 2021. "Mental Health and COVID-19 2021 Data." Mental Health America. Accessed on May 29, 2023. https://mhanational.org/mental-health-and-covid-19-april-2022-data.

Routledge. 2017. *The Psychology of Perfectionism: Theory, Research, Applications.* Edited by Joachim Stoeber. Publisher's Oxfordshire: Routledge.

A IS FOR AMBITION

Carucci, Ron. 2021. "How Ambitious Should You Be?" *Harvard Business Review* (blog). June 29, 2021. https://hbr.org/2020/04/how-ambitious-should-you-be.

Farnam Street. 2017. "David Foster Wallace: The Relationship Between Ambition and Perfectionism." *Farnam Street* (blog). April 17, 2017. https://fs.blog/david-foster-wallace-on-ambition-and-perfectionism/.

Ruggeri, Amanda. 2022. "The Dangerous Downsides of Perfectionism." *BBC Future* (blog). February 28, 2022. https://www.bbc.com/future/article/20180219-toxic-perfectionism-is-on-the-rise.

B IS FOR BEING THE BEST

Gino, Francesca. 2017. "The Problem with Being a Top Performer." *Scientific American* (blog). July 5, 2017. https://www.scientificamerican.com/article/the-problem-with-being-a-top-performer/.

Stanford University. 2021. "Your Powerful, Changeable Mindset—Stanford Report." Stanford Report. September 16, 2021. https://news.stanford.edu/report/2021/09/15/mindsets-clearing-lens-life/.

C IS FOR CONTROL

Food Allergy Research and Education. 2023. "Facts and Statistics." Accessed on May 29, 2023. https://www.foodallergy.org/resources/facts-and-statistics.

Hewett, Heather. 2014. "Food Allergies and the Good Enough Mother." *Allergic Living* (blog). October 9, 2014. https://www.allergicliving.com/2014/10/09/good-enough-mother/.

Theravive. 2023. "Perfectionism." *Theravive* (blog). Accessed on May 29, 2023. https://www.theravive.com/therapedia/perfectionism.

D IS FOR DISCOVERY

Cohen, Orna, and Rivka Savaya. 2004. "'Broken Glass': The Divorced Woman in Moslem Arab Society in Israel." *Family Process* 36, no. 3 (July): 225–45. https://doi. org/10.1111/j.1545-5300.1997.00225.x.

E IS FOR EMOTIONS

Adele, Teresa. 2023. "4 Expert-Backed Breathing Exercises for Anxiety." *Forbes Health* (blog). March 9, 2023. https:// www.forbes.com/health/mind/breathing-exercises-anxiety/.

Aldea, Mirela A. and Kenneth Rice. 2006. "The Role of Emotional Dysregulation in Perfectionism and Psychological Distress." *Journal of Counseling Psychology* 53, no. 4 (Oct): 498–510. https://doi.org/10.1037/0022-0167.53.4.498.

Brown, Harriet. 2013. "Looking For Evidence That Therapy Works." *The New York Times* (blog). March 25, 2013. https://archive.nytimes.com/well.blogs.nytimes. com/2013/03/25/looking-for-evidence-that-therapy-works/.

Davis, Tchiki. 2021. "What is Emotional Dysregulation?" *Psychology Today* (blog). August 23, 2021. https:// www.psychologytoday.com/us/blog/click-here-happiness/202108/what-is-emotional-dysregulation.

Garrity, Amanda and Lizz Schumer. 2022. "What Is a Bullet Journal? Everything You Need to Know Before You BuJo." *Good Housekeeping* (blog). February 11, 2022. https://www.

goodhousekeeping.com/life/a25940356/what-is-a-bullet-journal/.

LeGallo, Julia. 2021. "Perfectionism—The Battle of Never Feeling Quite Good Enough." Filmed January 2021 in Truro, Cornwall. TEDxTruro video, 11:19. https://www.ted.com/talks/julia_legallo_perfectionism_the_battle_of_never_feeling_quite_good_enough.

Rogers Behavioral Health. 2023. "Emotional Dysregulation Facts." *Rogers Behavioral Health* (blog). Accessed on May 29, 2023. https://rogersbh.org/emotional-dysregulation-facts.

F IS FOR FAILURE

Dweck, Carol S. 2006. *Mindset: The New Psychology of Success.* New York: Ballantine Books.

G IS FOR GOALS

Gardner, Sarah and Dave Albee. 2015. "Study Focuses on Strategies for Achieving Goals, Resolutions" *Dominican Scholar.* February 1, 2015. https://scholar.dominican.edu/news-releases/266.

Hess, Abigail Johnson. 2021. "'The Great Reimagination of Work': Why 50 percent of Workers Want to Make a Career Change." CNBC, October 12, 2021. https://www.cnbc.com/2021/10/12/why-50percent-of-workers-want-to-make-a-career-change-new-survey.html.

Nawaz, Sabina. 2020. "To Achieve Big Goals, Start with Small Habits." *Harvard Business Review* (blog). January 22, 2020.

https://hbr.org/2020/01/to-achieve-big-goals-start-with-small-habits?registration=success.

Pollak, Lindsey. 2021. *Recalculating: Navigate Your Career through the Changing World of Work*. New York City: HarperCollins.

H IS FOR HOPE

Ray, Julie. 2022. "World Unhappier, More Stressed Out Than Ever." *Gallup, Inc.* (blog). June 28, 2022. https://news. gallup.com/poll/394025/world-unhappier-stressed-ever. aspx.

I IS FOR IMPOSTOR SYNDROME

BBC News. 2018. "Michelle Obama: 'I Still Have Impostor Syndrome.'" BBC News, December 4, 2018. https://www. bbc.com/news/uk-46434147.

Leadem, Rose. 2017. "12 Leaders, Entrepreneurs and Celebrities Who Have Struggled with Imposter Syndrome." *Entrepreneur* (blog). November 8, 2017. https://www.entrepreneur.com/leadership/12-leaders-entrepreneurs-and-celebrities-who-have/304273.

Mainali, Sumina. 2020. "Being an Imposter: Growing Out of Impostership." *Journal of Nepal Medical Association* 58, no. 232 (Dec): 1097–1099. https://doi.org/10.31729/jnma.5505.

Nicols, Brittany. 2020. "Are You an Imposter?" *Innovate MR, LLC.* (blog). Accessed on May 29, 2023. https://blog. innovatemr.com/are-you-an-imposter?utm_source=PR_

Newswire&utm_medium=Press_Release&utm_
campaign=Release_2021.

Simpson, Jessica. 2020. *Open Book: A Memoir.* New York City:
HarperCollins.

Warrell, Margie. 2014. "Afraid of Being 'Found Out'?
How to Overcome Impostor Syndrome." *Forbes*
(blog). April 3, 2014. https://www.forbes.com/
sites/margiewarrell/2014/04/03/impostor-
syndrome/?sh=1566c36e48a9.

Weir, Kirsten. 2013. "Feel Like a Fraud?" *American
Psychological Association* (blog). November 2013. https://
www.apa.org/gradpsych/2013/11/fraud.

J IS FOR JOB

Aarons-Mele, Morra. 2022. "Digging Deeper on
Perfectionism." *The Anxious Achiever.* Released
November 16, 2022. 54 minutes. https://podcasts.apple.
com/ao/podcast/digging-deeper-on-perfectionism/
id1480904163?i=1000586457257.

Pollak, Lindsey. 2021. *Recalculating: Navigate Your Career
through the Changing World of Work.* New York City:
HarperCollins.

Swider, Brian, Dana Harari, Amy P. Breidenthal, and Laurens
Bujold Steed. 2021. "The Pros and Cons of Perfectionism,
According to Research." *Harvard Business Review* (blog).
September 17, 2021. https://hbr.org/2018/12/the-pros-and-
cons-of-perfectionism-according-to-research.

K IS FOR KIDS

Brown, Brené. 2010. "The Power of Vulnerability." Filmed December 2010 in Houston, TX. TEDxHouston video, 20:03. https://www.ted.com/talks/brene_brown_the_power_of_vulnerability/c?language=en.

Little, Celeste. 2022. "Exclusive: Michelle Obama Says It's up to Parents to Protect Black Children's Light." *Parents* (blog). November 30, 2022. https://www.parents.com/exclusive-michelle-obama-the-light-we-carry-6826469.

Newport Academy. 2022. "How Perfectionism in Children and Teens Impacts Mental Health." *Newport Academy* (blog). February 2, 2022. https://www.newportacademy.com/resources/empowering-teens/perfectionism-in-children/.

Rende, Richard. 2020. "I'm a Parent and a Psychologist: Here are 5 Signs of Low Self-Worth in Kids." *Parents* (blog). December 2, 2020. https://www.parents.com/parenting/better-parenting/advice/im-a-mom-and/im-a-dad-and-a-psychologist-these-are-the-signs-of-low-self-worth-in-kids-and-how-to-help/.

Waldman, Debby. 2022. "How to Help Your Kid Avoid Perfectionism." *Parents* (blog). June 13, 2022. https://www.parents.com/parenting/better-parenting/how-to-help-your-kid-avoid-perfectionism/.

Waters, Shonna. 2022. "Are You a Perfectionist? How to Understand What Is Causing It." *BetterUp* (blog). October 17, 2022. https://www.betterup.com/blog/what-causes-perfectionism.

L IS FOR LOVE

Doyle, Glennon. 2021. "Eff Perfection: Let's Rest in the Rubble Together." *We Can Do Hard Things*. Released December 22, 2021. 52 minutes. https://podcasts.apple.com/us/podcast/eff-perfection-lets-rest-in-the-rubble-together/id1564530722?i=1000545885422.

Economy, Peter. 2020. "How Perfectionism Tricks You into Downplaying Your Own Value." *Inc.Com* (blog). February 6, 2020. https://www.inc.com/peter-economy/how-perfectionism-tricks-you-into-downplaying-your-own-value.html.

Fang, Tingting and Fan Liu. 2022. "A Review on Perfectionism." *Open Journal of Social Sciences* 10, no. 1: 355–364. https://doi.org/10.4236/jss.2022.101027.

LeGallo, Julia. 2021. "Perfectionism—The Battle of Never Feeling Quite Good Enough." Filmed January 2021 in Truro, Cornwall. TEDxTruro video, 11:19. https://www.ted.com/talks/julia_legallo_perfectionism_the_battle_of_never_feeling_quite_good_enough.

National Organization for Women. 2014. "Get the Facts | National Organization for Women." *National Organization for Women* (blog). Accessed on June 2, 2023. https://now.org/now-foundation/love-your-body/love-your-body-whats-it-all-about/get-the-facts/.

Simpson, Jessica. 2020. *Open Book*. New York City: HarperCollins.

The Aesthetic Society. 2022. "The Aesthetic Society Releases Annual Statistics Revealing Significant Increases in Face,

Breast and Body in 2021." *The Aesthetic Society* (blog).
Accessed on June 2, 2023. https://www.theaestheticsociety.
org/media/press-releases/aesthetic-society-releases-
annual-statistics-revealing-significant-increases.

M IS FOR MISTAKES

Aarons-Mele, Morra. 2022. "Digging Deeper on
Perfectionism." *The Anxious Achiever.* Released
November 16, 2022. 54 minutes. https://podcasts.apple.
com/ao/podcast/digging-deeper-on-perfectionism/
id1480904163?i=1000586457257.

Boyes, Alice. 2020. "How to Overcome Your Fear of Making
Mistakes." *Harvard Business Review* (blog). June 29, 2020.
https://hbr.org/2020/06/how-to-overcome-your-fear-of-
making-mistakes.

Fang, Tingting and Fan Liu. 2022. "A Review on
Perfectionism." *Open Journal of Social Sciences* 10, no. 1:
355–64. https://doi.org/10.4236/jss.2022.101027.

Mark, Clifton. 2019. "You're Afraid of the Wrong Things:
What Evolution Made You Scared of versus What
Actually Might Kill You." *CBC* (blog). April 5, 2019.
https://www.cbc.ca/life/culture/you-re-afraid-of-the-
wrong-things-what-evolution-made-you-scared-of-
versus-what-actually-might-kill-you-1.5086576.

N IS FOR NATURE

Fang, Tingting and Fan Liu. 2022. "A Review on
Perfectionism." *Open Journal of Social Sciences* 10, no. 1:
355–64. https://doi.org/10.4236/jss.2022.101027.

Laskowski, Edward. 2022. "What are the Risks of Sitting Too Much?" *Mayo Clinic* (blog). July 13, 2022. https://www. mayoclinic.org/healthy-lifestyle/adult-health/expert-answers/sitting/faq-20058005.

Pritchard, Alison E., Miles Richardson, David Sheffield, and Kirsten McEwan. 2020. "The Relationship Between Nature Connectedness and Eudaimonic Well-Being: A Meta-Analysis." *Journal of Happiness Studies* 21, no.3: 1145–67. https://doi.org/10.1007/s10902-019-00118-6.

Weir, Kirsten. 2020. "Nurtured by Nature." *Monitor on Psychology* 51, no. 3. https://www.apa.org/ monitor/2020/04/nurtured-nature.

O IS FOR OVERACHIEVER

DeLong, Thomas J. and Sara DeLong. 2014. "Managing Yourself: The Paradox of Excellence." *Harvard Business Review* (blog). August 1, 2014. https://hbr.org/2011/06/ managing-yourself-the-paradox-of-excellence.

Eldad, Keren. 2019. "4 Ways Overachievers Are Sabotaging Their Own Career—and How They Can Change That." *CNBC*, September 15, 2019. https://www.cnbc. com/2019/09/15/4-ways-overachievers-are-sabotaging-their-career-how-they-can-stop.html.

Eldad, Keren. 2019. "The Superstar Paradox—How Overachievers Miss the Mark in Life and at Work." *Journal of Psychology Research* 9, no.8. https://doi. org/10.17265/2159-5542/2019.08.005.

Enten, Harry. 2022. "American Happiness Hits Record Lows." *CNN*, February 2, 2022. https://www.cnn.com/2022/02/02/politics/unhappiness-americans-gallup-analysis/index.html.

Gingerella, Benita. 2022. "Over Half of Today's College Students Report Feeling Lonely, Sodexo Survey Reveals." *FoodService Director* (blog). August 16, 2022. https://www.foodservicedirector.com/operations/over-half-todays-college-students-report-feeling-lonely-sodexo-survey-reveals.

P IS FOR PROCRASTINATION AND PARALYSIS

Aarons-Mele, Morra. 2022. "Digging Deeper on Perfectionism." *The Anxious Achiever.* Released November 16, 2022. 54 minutes. https://podcasts.apple.com/ao/podcast/digging-deeper-on-perfectionism/id1480904163?i=1000586457257.

Flett, Gordon L., Paul Hewitt, and Thomas R. Martin. 1995. "Dimensions of Perfectionism and Procrastination." In *Procrastination and Task Avoidance.* 113–136. Springer, Boston: The Springer Series in Social Clinical Psychology.

Lieberman, Charlotte. 2019. "Why You Procrastinate (It Has Nothing to Do With Self-Control)." *The New York Times*, March 27, 2019. https://www.nytimes.com/2019/03/25/smarter-living/why-you-procrastinate-it-has-nothing-to-do-with-self-control.html.

Reclaim.ai, Inc. 2022. "Task Management Trends Report: +200 Stats on Managers vs. Individual Contributors | Reclaim."

Reclaim.ai, Inc. (blog). March 29, 2022. https://reclaim.ai/
blog/task-management-trends-report.

Reclaim.ai, Inc. 2022. "What Is Decision Paralysis? How
to Prevent in 4 Steps | Reclaim." *Reclaim.ai, Inc.* (blog).
April 18, 2022. https://reclaim.ai/blog/prevent-decision-
paralysis.

Sinek, Simon. 2022. "Two Bits of Optimism with Brené Brown
and Adam Grant: Part One." *A Bit of Optimism.* Released
December 13, 2022. 38 minutes. https://simonsinek.com/
podcast/episodes/two-bits-of-optimism-with-brene-
brown-and-adam-grant-part-one/.

TEDx Talks. 2015. "Tales of a Recovering Perfectionist |
Adrianne Haslet-Davis | TEDxStLouisWomen." TEDx
Talks. Jun 3, 2015. 18:28. https://www.youtube.com/
watch?v=PCaKHuirmY8.

Q IS FOR QUESTION EVERYTHING

Galbin, Alexandra. 2014. "An Introduction to Social
Constructionism." *Social Research Reports* 26 (2014): 82–92.
https://www.researchreports.ro/images/researchreports/
social/srr_2014_vol026_004.pdf.

McNamee, Sheila. 2010. "Research as Social Construction:
Transformative Inquiry." *Saúde & Transformação Social* 1,
no.1: 09–19. https://incubadora.periodicos.ufsc.br/index.
php/saudeetransformacao/article/view/418/477.

National Network of Depression Centers. 2018. "Get the
Facts—National Network of Depression Centers."

National Network of Depression Centers, August 22, 2018. https://nndc.org/facts.

R IS FOR RELATIONSHIPS

Borreli, Lizette. 2016. "People-Pleaser: Brain Scans Show Pushovers Agree with Others to Avoid Mental Stress." *Medical Daily* (blog). March 2, 2016. https://www.medicaldaily.com/people-pleaser-brain-activity-mental-stress-376139.

Edwards, Scott. 2015. "Love and the Brain." *Harvard Medical School* (blog). Spring 2015. https://hms.harvard.edu/news-events/publications-archive/brain/love-brain.

Finch, Sam Dylan. 2019. "How to Tell If People-Pleasing Is a Trauma Response." *Healthline* (blog). September 30, 2019. https://www.healthline.com/health/mental-health/7-subtle-signs-your-trauma-response-is-people-pleasing.

S IS FOR SOCIAL MEDIA

Anderson, Monica. 2018. "A Majority of Teens Have Experienced Some Form of Cyberbullying | Pew Research Center." *Pew Research Center* (blog). September 27, 2018. https://www.pewresearch.org/internet/2018/09/27/a-majority-of-teens-have-experienced-some-form-of-cyberbullying/.

Anderson, Monica, Emily A. Vogels, Andres Perrin, and Lee Rainie. 2022. "Connection, Creativity and Drama: Teen Life on Social Media in 2022 | Pew Research Center." *Pew Research Center* (blog). November 17, 2022. https://

www.pewresearch.org/internet/2022/11/16/connection-creativity-and-drama-teen-life-on-social-media-in-2022/.

Aschwanden, Christie. 2019. "Perfectionism Is Killing Us." *Vox* (blog). December 5, 2019. https://www.vox.com/the-highlight/2019/11/27/20975989/perfect-mental-health-perfectionism.

Holcombe, Madeline. 2022. "Teens Say Their Experience on Social Media Is Better than You Think. Here's Why." *CNN*, November 16, 2022. https://www.cnn.com/2022/11/16/health/teens-social-media-pew-survey-wellness.

Murphy Kelly, Samantha. 2022. "Their Teenage Children Died by Suicide. Now These Families Want to Hold Social Media Companies Accountable." *CNN Business* (blog). April 19, 2022. https://www.cnn.com/2022/04/19/tech/social-media-lawsuits-teen-suicide/index.html.

Shabnoor, Siddiqui and Tajinder Singh. 2016. "Social Media Its Impact with Positive and Negative Aspects." *International Journal of Computer Applications Technology and Research* 5, no. 2: 71–75. https://jogamayadevicollege.ac.in/uploads/1586197536.pdf.

Wike, Richard, Laura Silver, Janelle Fetterolf, Christine Huang, Sarah Austin, Laura Clancy, and Sneha Gubbala. 2022. "Social Media Seen as Mostly Good for Democracy across Many Nations, but US Is a Major Outlier | Pew Research Center." *Pew Research Center* (blog). December 6, 2022. https://www.pewresearch.org/global/2022/12/06/social-media-seen-as-mostly-good-for-democracy-across-many-nations-but-u-s-is-a-major-outlier/.

T IS FOR TIME

John, Steven. 2019. "7 Ways American Work Habits Have Changed in the Past 10 Years." *Business Insider* (blog). March 27, 2019. https://www.businessinsider.com/american-work-habits-culture-change-2019-3.

Main, Kelly. 2023. "The Hidden Problem with Perfectionism— and How Anyone Can Use This Solution to Feel More Fulfilled." *Inc.Com* (blog). January 23, 2023. https://www.inc.com/kelly-main/the-hidden-problem-with-perfectionism-and-how-anyone-can-use-this-solution-to-feel-more-fulfilled.html.

Sollinger, Marc. 2016. "The Invention of Time." *GBH News* (blog). February 15, 2016. https://www.wgbh.org/news/2016/02/15/innovation/invention-time.

U IS FOR UNDERESTIMATE

Aragão, Carolina. 2023. "Gender Pay Gap in US Hasn't Changed Much in Two Decades | Pew Research Center." *Pew Research Center* (blog). March 1, 2023. https://www.pewresearch.org/fact-tank/2021/05/25/gender-pay-gap-facts/.

Kay, Katty and Claire Shipman. 2015. "The Confidence Gap." *The Atlantic* (blog). August 26, 2015. https://www.theatlantic.com/magazine/archive/2014/05/the-confidence-gap/359815/.

V IS FOR VULNERABILITY

Balch, Bridget. 2021. "There Is No Courage without Vulnerability." AAMC, November 9, 2021. https://www.

aamc.org/news-insights/there-no-courage-without-vulnerability.

Blumberg, Yoni. 2018. "Being Vulnerable Can Make You More Successful at Work—Here's How." *CNBC*, March 19, 2018. https://www.cnbc.com/2018/03/19/vulnerability-can-make-you-more-successful.html.

Brown, Brené. 2010. "The Power of Vulnerability." Filmed December 2010 in Houston, TX. TEDxHouston video, 20:03. https://www.ted.com/talks/brene_brown_the_power_of_vulnerability?language=en.

Harter, Jim. 2023. "US Employee Engagement Slump Continues." *Gallup Inc.* (blog). April 19, 2023. https://www.gallup.com/workplace/391922/employee-engagement-slump-continues.aspx.

W IS FOR WEIGHT

Grand View Research, Inc. 2023. "Cosmetic Surgery and Procedure Market Size, Share & Trends Analysis Report by Type (Invasive, Non-Invasive), Region (North America, Asia Pacific, Middle East & Africa, Latin America, Europe), and Segment Forecasts, 2022—2030." Grand View Research, Inc. Accessed on June 2, 2023. https://www.grandviewresearch.com/industry-analysis/cosmetic-surgery-procedure-market.

Levine, Michael and Sarah K. Murnen. 2009. "'Everybody Knows That Mass Media Are/Are Not [*Pick One*] a Cause of Eating Disorders': A Critical Review of Evidence for a Causal Link Between Media, Negative Body Image, and Disordered Eating in Females." *Journal of Social and*

Clinical Psychology 28, no.1: 9–42. https://doi.org/10.1521/jscp.2009.28.1.9.

National Eating Disorders Association. 2021. "Statistics & Research on Eating Disorders." National Eating Disorders Association, July 14, 2021. https://www.nationaleatingdisorders.org/statistics-research-eating-disorders.

Willer, Sarah. 2017. *The 2017 Dove Global Girls Beauty and Confidence Report.* London: Dove.

X IS FOR EXPECTATIONS

American Psychological Association. 2022. "Rising Parental Expectations Linked to Perfectionism in College Students." *American Psychological Association* (blog). March 31, 2022. https://www.apa.org/news/press/releases/2022/03/parental-expectations-perfectionism.

Indeed Editorial Team. 2022. "How to Set Realistic Goals." *Indeed. Com* (blog). July 5, 2022. https://www.indeed.com/career-advice/career-development/how-to-set-realistic-goals.

Jern, Alan, PhD. 2023. "The Power of Low Expectations." *Psychology Today* (blog). January 26, 2023. https://www.psychologytoday.com/us/blog/overthinking-tv/202301/the-power-of-low-expectations.

Moss, Jennifer. 2020. "Why Ditching High Expectations Now Could Lead To More Happiness Later." *CBC*, April 26, 2020. https://www.cbc.ca/news/canada/kitchener-waterloo/jennifer-moss-happiness-column-lower-expectations-1.5544290.

Pollak, Lindsey. 2021. *Recalculating: Navigate Your Career through the Changing World of Work*. New York City: HarperCollins.

Y IS FOR YESTERDAY

Aschwanden, Christie. 2019. "Perfectionism Is Killing Us." *Vox* (blog). December 5, 2019. https://www.vox.com/the-highlight/2019/11/27/20975989/perfect-mental-health-perfectionism.

Doyle, Glennon. 2021. "Eff Perfection: Let's Rest in the Rubble Together." *We Can Do Hard Things*. Released December 22, 2021. 52 minutes. https://podcasts.apple.com/us/podcast/eff-perfection-lets-rest-in-the-rubble-together/id1564530722?i=1000545885422.

Jurkschat, Jessica. 2022. "Number of Informed Decisions We Make per Day Revealed in New Research." *Yahoo* (blog). August 9, 2022. https://www.yahoo.com/lifestyle/number-of-decisions-we-make-daily-revealed-102938055.html.

Krockow, Eva M., PhD. 2019. "How Many Decisions Do We Make Each Day?" *Psychology Today* (blog). December 29, 2019. https://www.psychologytoday.com/us/blog/stretching-theory/201809/how-many-decisions-do-we-make-each-day.

Z IS FOR ZOOM

Aarons-Mele, Morra. 2022. "Digging Deeper on Perfectionism." *The Anxious Achiever*. Released November 16, 2022. 54 minutes. https://podcasts.apple.

com/ao/podcast/digging-deeper-on-perfectionism/
id1480904163?i=1000586457257.

Brooks, Arthur C. 2022. "The Trouble with Zooming Forever."
The Atlantic, July 14, 2022. https://www.theatlantic.
com/family/archive/2022/07/how-to-fight-zoom-
fatigue/670513/.

Grand View Research, Inc. 2023. "Cosmetic Surgery and
Procedure Market Size, Share & Trends Analysis Report
by Type (Invasive, Non-Invasive), Region (North America,
Asia Pacific, Middle East & Africa, Latin America,
Europe), and Segment Forecasts, 2022–2030." Grand View
Research, Inc. Accessed on June 2, 2023. https://www.
grandviewresearch.com/industry-analysis/cosmetic-
surgery-procedure-market.

Ramachandran, Vignesh. 2021. "Stanford Researcher Identify
Four Causes for 'Zoom Fatigue' and Their Simple Fixes" |
Stanford News. February 23, 2021. https://news.stanford.
edu/2021/02/23/four-causes-zoom-fatigue-solutions/.